To:

_____

From:

_____

Message:

_____

_____

101 ADVENTURES WITH GOD

LIZETTE MURRAY

christian art kids

Hi there!

Life with Jesus is not boring at all! It's an adventure! A series of wonderful experiences.

God invites you to take your backpack and go on this exciting adventure with Him.

Enjoy the ride!

I look up to the mountains – does my help come from there? My help comes from the Lord, who made heaven and earth! He will not let you stumble; the one who watches over you will not slumber. Indeed, He who watches over Israel never slumbers or sleeps. The Lord Himself watches over you! The Lord stands beside you as your protective shade. The sun will not harm you by day, nor the moon at night. The Lord keeps you from all harm and watches over your life. The Lord keeps watch over you as you come and go, both now and forever.

Psalm 121
A Song for Pilgrims Ascending to Jerusalem

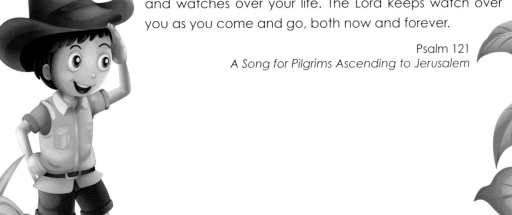

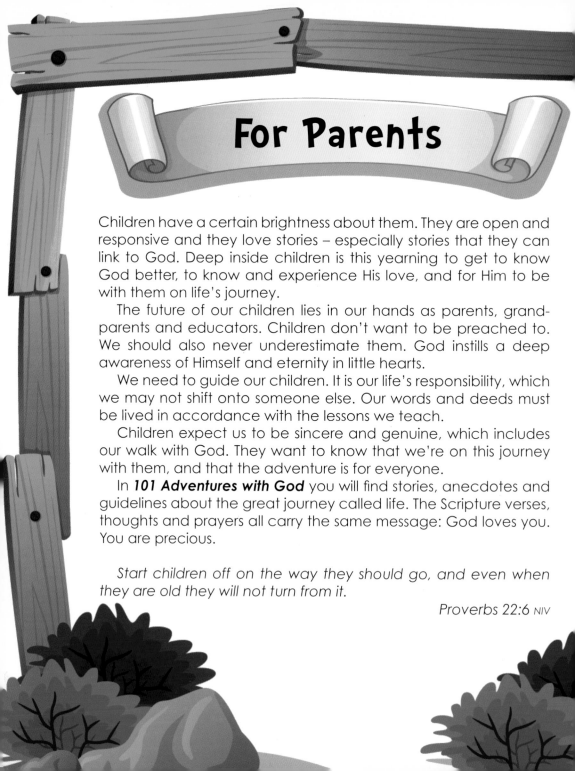

For Parents

Children have a certain brightness about them. They are open and responsive and they love stories – especially stories that they can link to God. Deep inside children is this yearning to get to know God better, to know and experience His love, and for Him to be with them on life's journey.

The future of our children lies in our hands as parents, grandparents and educators. Children don't want to be preached to. We should also never underestimate them. God instills a deep awareness of Himself and eternity in little hearts.

We need to guide our children. It is our life's responsibility, which we may not shift onto someone else. Our words and deeds must be lived in accordance with the lessons we teach.

Children expect us to be sincere and genuine, which includes our walk with God. They want to know that we're on this journey with them, and that the adventure is for everyone.

In **101 Adventures with God** you will find stories, anecdotes and guidelines about the great journey called life. The Scripture verses, thoughts and prayers all carry the same message: God loves you. You are precious.

Start children off on the way they should go, and even when they are old they will not turn from it.

Proverbs 22:6 NIV

Acknowledgment

During the course of your life you read or hear stories that stay with you. Some of the stories in *101 Adventures with God* are from my own childhood treasury of stories. I came across some in newspapers, magazines and via the Internet. Some were conveyed to me verbally. Some are my own writings. The origin of others I do not know. I wrote it as I recalled it.

Contents

Scary Stuff

You and Your Teammates

God Walks Before Us

Packing Checklist

You need a backpack to go on a journey.
Pack a map, binoculars and food for
your adventure with God.

God's Word is your map. In the Bible He tells you exactly which way to go every day.

Your food is your quiet times with God when you talk to Him – and when He talks to you.

Your binoculars help you to see farther than today ... Your binocular's name is **Faith and Hope.**

Your word is a lamp to guide my feet and a light for my path. Psalm 119:105

A Good Adventure

"I am the light of the world. If you follow Me, you won't have to walk in darkness, because you will have the light that leads to life." John 8:12

We all love an adventure. Some people like surfing; others like mountain climbing or camping, or riding their bikes. Then there are some who like the adventure of reading a book or seeing a movie. Adventure is something that brightens up a dull and boring day!

A group of boys went camping with their dads close to a river. When it became dark, they built a fire. They sang songs around the campfire. Then they started telling ghost stories. The boys crept up close beside their fathers and every now and then glanced into the dark forest to make sure nothing was lurking there.

The bigger boys wanted to show how brave they were and decided to go for a walk along the river. They disappeared between the thick bushes. At first you could hear their voices. Later only the night sounds could be heard. The group waiting by the fire suddenly heard anxious cries and screams.

A little while later the boys shyly reappeared in the dark. The "ghost" that had frightened them was a black cow bellowing at them for disturbing her!

"Why didn't you take your torches along?" asked one of the small boys. "Then you would've seen the cow!"

As easy as that! When the light shines, everything looks so much better!

Lord Jesus, thank You for being the Light on my path. Thank You that I don't ever have to be afraid when I live in Your light. Amen.

Yellow Markers

Your own ears will hear Him. Right behind you a voice
will say, "This is the way you should go." Isaiah 30:21

A group of boys were invited to attend a pirate-themed party. The birthday boy's mom went to the camp site the day before and placed yellow arrows all along the foot path. Then she hid a big metal trunk filled with party treats and prizes. At each marker she hid a note under a rock. On the note she wrote a clue, almost like on the TV show *Survivor*. On the last note she wrote:

→ Follow the arrow to the gate.

→ You've almost found the hiding place.

→ Walk ten steps farther along the path.

→ Under the bushes you will find the treasure.

And there under the thick bushes lay the hidden trunk with the treats.

Some of the boys were in such a hurry to get to the treasure chest that they missed some of the arrows. They went to look for the treasure in the wrong place. The boy's mom had to tell them, "Go back to the previous arrow and read the note carefully."

Eventually all the party members reached the trunk and celebrated together!

God directs our path through life. His Word is our yellow markers that tell us: "Walk this way." The words from the Bible are like the notes hidden under the rocks that tell us how to live our lives so that we can also find the "treasure chest of eternal life." And then we can celebrate with Jesus!

Lord Jesus, thank You for showing me which
way to go in life so that I don't get lost. Amen.

Rock Climbing

Grow in the grace and knowledge of our Lord and Savior Jesus Christ. 2 Peter 3:18

Have you seen how mountain climbers creep up rocky cliffs like little geckos? First, they choose their steps carefully. Then they look for sharp rocks or pinnacles with which to pull themselves up.

Sometimes they go really slowly, especially when they're climbing a sheer cliff. Fortunately they have ropes and harnesses to keep them safe. The hooks are hammered into the rocks beforehand so that they can tie the ropes to them in order to anchor themselves.

A new rock climber said to his team leader, "If I stay on the ground and watch the others climb, I will know what to do."

"But then you will never learn to climb," replied the leader. "Start at the bottom and take one step at a time. Then pull yourself up. That is how you practice and learn how to rock climb – not by watching others."

Our faith can only grow stronger when we practice. We can't stand on the sideline, too scared to make a mistake.

Exercise your faith muscles. God is your leader! He goes before you.

Lord, help me to grow and become strong in the faith. Amen.

Have you ever tried indoor rock climbing? Ask your mom if there is a place nearby and try it!

The Desert Rose

I rejoice in Your word like one who
discovers a great treasure. Psalm 119:162

Sally had to do a school assignment about desert roses. She had never heard of them and was already feeling discouraged. She didn't know where to start. First she asked her older sister if she knew anything about the topic, but she only shrugged her shoulders. Then she asked her mom. Mom said she should look it up in an encyclopedia, but they didn't have one at home. Dad told her he didn't have time to help.

Sally felt like she would never find the answers, no matter how hard she tried!

But then she typed the words "desert rose" into Google on her computer. On the screen appeared the most beautiful and vibrant images of flowers that grow in the desert. She read that desert roses can form crystal clusters through sandstorms in the desert. The clusters look like flower petals. There was even a song called *Desert Rose!*

Sally was very excited about everything she had learned. The answers were there all along – she just had to look for them in the right place.

The Bible is our manual for life, filled with all the answers. If we live according to what the Bible says, we will never get lost. We must just open our Bibles and start reading.

Lord, thank You for Your Word that gives me the answers about how I should live. Help me to read the Bible every day. Amen.

Did you know that Psalm 119 is the longest chapter in the whole Bible? Every verse tells us something about God's Word.

Covered in Glitter!

When Moses came down Mount Sinai carrying the two stone tablets inscribed with the terms of the covenant, he wasn't aware that his face had become radiant because he had spoken to the LORD. Exodus 34:29

It's party time! Taylor's mom baked him an amazing racing car cake. She sprinkled glitter over the blue icing. After Taylor blew out the candles, Mom cut the cake and everybody had a slice. When they looked up from eating their cake, everyone started laughing. Their mouths were covered in glitter!

When Moses received the two tablets of stone from God with the Ten Commandments written on them, His face shone brightly. When he came down the mountain to the people, they could see that Moses had been with God. But he didn't know that his face was shining.

In the same way, others can see if you're a child of God and you love Him. It rubs off on you – just like the glitter on the children's faces after they ate the birthday cake.

When children love Jesus, He teaches them not to get angry quickly. He teaches them to be patient and to say only kind things about others. Jesus' children have respect for their parents and teachers.

It's not always easy, is it? We don't always get it right. Therefore, it is very important to spend time with God – just like Moses did.

Lord, I want to talk to You every day. I also want to read Your Word daily so that I can reflect Your love and kindness to others. Amen.

Rock Solid

"When someone comes to Me, listens to My teaching, and then follows it … It is like a person building a house who digs deep and lays the foundation on solid rock. When the floodwaters rise and break against that house, it stands firm because it is well built." Luke 6:47-48

At the beach, children like to build sandcastles. Sometimes they build very beautiful castles. First they dig a trench right around so that the water can't reach the castle. Then they build the castle in the middle. Usually the castle has many towers. You can also decorate it with sea shells. It is so much fun!

The children laugh and tell each other how strong their castle is. But then, out of nowhere, a big wave washes the castle away!

In the Bible we read about two men. One wanted to build his house on the sand; the other man on a rock. When a storm and floodwaters came, the house on the sand collapsed in a heap, while the house on the rock stood firm.

From far off, the houses might have looked similar. The difference was that the house on the rock had a firm and deep foundation.

When things go well, people all seem the same. They are friendly and help others and don't get upset. But when things don't go so well, you can see who serves God, and who lives without Him.

A person who knows the Lord is like the man who built his house on a rock.

Lord Jesus, I want to listen to Your commands
and live like You want me to. Please help me. Amen.

Do you know the Ten
Commandments in Exodus 20?
Try to learn them off by heart.

Kite Flying

Never stop praying, especially for others. Always
pray by the power of the Spirit. Stay alert and
keep praying for God's people. Ephesians 6:18 CEV

Have you ever tried flying a kite? It's not so easy. Sometimes the wind is not strong enough – then the kite only whirls in the sky and falls straight back to the ground. At other times the wind is too strong – then the wind tugs at the kite until it dives to the ground. Or your string can get tied up, or the kite can get stuck in a tree.

Our prayers are like a kite: When we don't feel like praying, our prayers don't want to take off. We don't think about what we're praying, and only recite our prayers like a poem before bedtime.

At other times we rush our prayers. Then it's like a kite that dives into the ground. That's not a true prayer – it's just a bunch of words. It makes the Lord sad when we talk to Him like this without giving Him a chance to also speak to us.

When our thoughts wander to the sports match or party coming up, then we get tied up like the string of the kite.

Jesus wants our prayers to rise high up in the sky like a beautiful kite. He is our Father who holds our hands while our prayer kites rise. He also wants to teach us how to pray, just like He taught His disciples the Lord's Prayer.

Lord Jesus, please teach me how to pray. I really want
to talk to You and not just repeat a bunch of words. Amen.

Do you know the Lord's Prayer by heart?

Sweet Incense

*Each one had a harp, and they held gold bowls filled
with incense, which are the prayers of God's people. Revelation 5:8*

When Jesus was born, one of the wise men brought Him incense as a gift. Incense is very precious. When you hold it in your hand, it's just a black lump. But when you light it, it releases white smoke, and the smell fills the whole room.

In biblical times the priests burned incense in the temple. It was an offering to God to praise Him because He is so wonderful. Incense was one of the ways they could bring an offering to the Lord.

In Revelation it says that our prayers are like incense rising up to God. It doesn't matter if we have sinned. When we pray with sincere hearts, the sweet smell of our prayers rise up to God like the white smoke of pure incense. When we don't pray, we just stay a black lump that doesn't smell nice.

Dear Father, even if my prayers are not perfect,
I know that You hear every word and that my
prayers rise up to You like a sweet perfume. Amen.

Just Ask!

Now all glory to God, who is able to accomplish
infinitely more than we might ask or think. Ephesians 3:20

In Josh's street there was a house with a big apricot tree. From his bedroom window, Josh could see the golden fruit. But he didn't want to pick the fruit without the owner's permission.

One day Josh and his friend Andy were playing in the garden. Andy saw the apricots on the tree next door and wanted one. "Let's knock on the door and ask if we can pick a few apricots," Andy suggested.

Josh was a bit shy and cautious. "I'm scared the owner will be cross. No, let's just leave it." But Andy was already out the door and running to the house next door.

The neighbor was friendly and invited the two boys in. "You can pick apricots any time. Just don't break the branches or fall out the tree," she said in a friendly voice, "and don't pick the plums; they're not yet ripe."

A little while later she brought them a basket. "Pick some for your mom as well," she said. The two boys couldn't believe it. They got even more than they'd hoped for!

"You see!" said Andy, "if you don't ask, you get nothing!"

Dear Father, I know that everything belongs
to You. You know what is good for us, but You
still want us to ask You for the things we need. Amen.

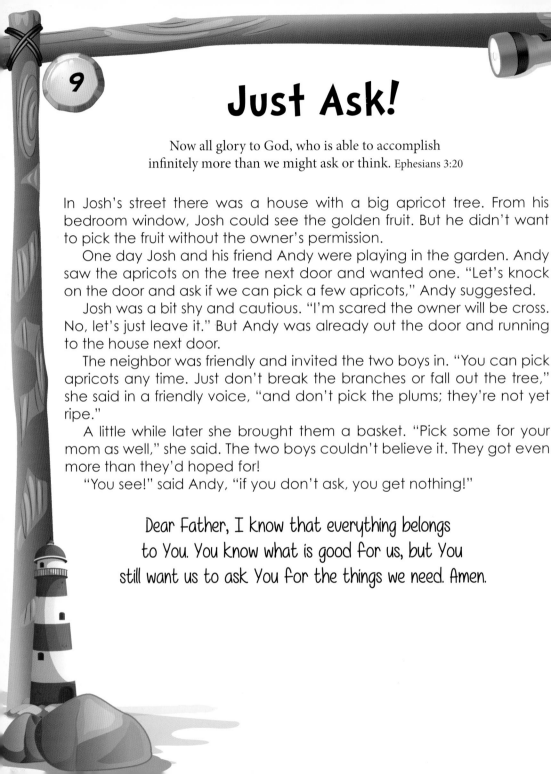

The Traffic Light

"Your Father knows what you need before you ask Him." Matthew 6:8 NIV

Sometimes you pray and pray, but it doesn't feel like God listens or hears your prayers. It might feel like He has turned His face away from you, or that your needs are not important enough to Him.

God answers all our prayers, even if we don't always think so. We must just listen carefully.

Our heavenly Father's answers are like a traffic light: Red. Yellow. Green.

Sometimes He says, "Yes, My child, I will give you what you ask for." Then it's like a green traffic light that says, "You can go. It's safe."

At other times He says, "Wait a bit. I'll give you an answer later. The time is not right. I want you to be patient." Then the Lord's answer is like the yellow light that says, "Steady now. Be patient."

But sometimes the Lord says, "No, I can't give you what you're asking for. It won't be good for you."

And that is His final answer. It's like a red traffic light that says: "Stop". Oh! It's hard to hear that "No!"

Dear Father, thank You for knowing
what is best for me. Help me to trust
in You – even when You say no. Amen.

Read the next devotion to
find out more about a "red
traffic light" answer to prayer.

God's Purposes Will Prevail

We know that God causes everything to work together for the good of those who love God and are called according to His purpose for them. Romans 8:28

Many years ago in the Netherlands there lived a girl named Mariecke. All her friends in Holland had blonde hair and blue eyes. She was the only one who didn't. She wished every day that she could look more like the others.

One Sunday the pastor read the following Scripture verse: "Keep on asking, and you will receive what you ask for" (Matthew 7:7). *Aha!* Mariecke thought. *It's just what I needed to hear.*

Every evening she prayed for her eyes to become blue and her hair blonde. But every morning she looked the same. Eventually she stopped praying because she decided it wasn't helping.

Many years later Mariecke became a missionary in Iraq. She had to wear a burqa like all the other women. A burqa is a long black garment that covers you from head to toe with the exception of your eyes.

It was dangerous being a Christian in Iraq. The Christians were persecuted and thrown in jail. One day, Mariecke was strolling in the market place when she saw some soldiers. Suddenly she realized how lucky she was to have dark eyes and dark hair. She looked just like all the others. She remembered how she had prayed for blue eyes. She realized that the Lord always knows what is best for His children.

Dear Lord who protects me, sometimes I get angry when You don't give me what I want. Only afterwards do I realize that You had good reason to not say yes. Please remind me that You know what is best. Amen.

It Is Good to Wait

12

His glorious power will make you patient and strong enough
to endure anything, and you will be truly happy. Colossians 1:11 CEV

"Why can't I get my bike today, Dad?" asked James. "Because your birthday is only the day after tomorrow, my boy."

"But, Dad! Two days is *very* long! Pleeease! I'll just ride around the block and then I'll put it back in the garage."

"We've talked about this. My answer is no. You must learn to be patient."

Then James decided to do something else so that the time could pass by quickly. He decided to tidy the garage. First he picked up all the rubbish lying around and put it in a bag.

The next day after school he wiped down all the shelves and cleaned the paint brushes and buckets. Then he washed the floor.

James felt pleased. Everything was clean and tidy. He looked at his watch. It was almost seven o'clock. He couldn't believe how fast the day had gone by. Tomorrow was going to be his birthday!

The next morning when James opened his eyes, something was already standing by his bed. A brand-new bicycle! His heart was beating fast from excitement. He was glad that he waited patiently. This bright, shiny new bicycle would not have been so special if his dad had given it to him two days early.

James learned a valuable lesson: Sometimes it *is* good to wait!

Lord, I often become impatient when I ask
for something. You are the best Father.
You know exactly what I need. Please
help me to wait patiently. Amen.

A Handful of Prayers

The Lord watches over everyone who obeys Him,
and He listens to their prayers. 1 Peter 3:12 CEV

We don't always know where to start when we pray. There are so many things to pray for that sometimes we get tired thinking of everyone and everything. Then we just repeat the same words.

There is an easy way to help you. Think about your hand and its five fingers. Each finger looks different. If you think about a different finger every night, you'll have many different things to pray about.

Your thumb is closest to your body. With your thumb prayer you can pray for the people closest to you: your parents, brothers and sisters, grandparents, cousins, aunts and uncles. And your best friends.

On the next night you pray index finger prayers – all the people who teach others, like teachers and pastors. Pray that they will receive wisdom from God.

Your middle finger is the longest finger. This represents leaders. Pray for the leaders of your church, school and country. They all need God's help.

The fourth finger is your ring finger. Here you pray for marriages. Pray that God will protect your mom and dad's love for each other. If your parents are divorced, you can pray that the Lord will help to heal their hearts.

Your little finger prayer is for all the people who are unable to take care of themselves. This includes small children, sick people, old people and poor people.

The Lord wants us to pray for each other.

Dear Lord, help me to faithfully pray for other people, using my five fingers. Amen.

Soaring High

Those who trust in the LORD will find new strength. They will soar high on wings like eagles. They will run and not grow weary. They will walk and not faint. Isaiah 40:31

Have you ever wished you could fly?

I think all of us at one time or another wish that we could fly – to feel free and soar in the sky. We think that we can escape from everyone and everything. The birds look like they have no cares in the world when they fly way up high.

But we *can* fly. Not with wings, but with our thoughts. When we've had a bad day at school or at home, we can escape to God in our thoughts. We can talk to Him and tell Him about everything that is bothering us. He will help us to feel more at peace, even though the world is still the same.

When you feel alone and tired, go and lie on the grass and look up at the night sky. Think about how great and powerful God is. He is the Ruler of the skies and the animals. He cares for everything, great and small, and especially for you.

Spread your wings and fly with Him.

Lord, help me to come to You when everything seems too much to handle. Thank You for renewing my strength! You make me soar like an eagle. Amen.

Have you ever laid on your back and looked at the clouds in the sky? It is then that you realize: God is great!

Time for the Lord

Then Jesus returned to the disciples and found them asleep. He said
to Peter, "Couldn't you watch with Me even one hour?" Matthew 26:40

The other day I read a piece from a diary that someone wrote in
1875. It said:

"It's busy on the farm. The whole morning we were busy breaking
open apricots to put them on the drying racks in the sun. This afternoon
I sewed the buttons onto my dress. Forty buttons altogether. I'm very
busy. I have so little time to read and pray!"

It seems like the people in previous centuries were just as busy as
we are. However, we tend to think that we are busier than ever! We
certainly don't have time to sew forty buttons onto a dress. We buy
our dresses and quickly zip them up.

Today we can get much more done in less time. We have
computers that can send e-mails quickly. We have smartphones,
laptops, cars and airplanes.

Whether we lived a hundred years ago or today, we fill our days
with things to do. And we are just as tired at the end of a long day
as the people were ages ago.

Do you make time for the Lord in your busy day? He is the same
as He was a hundred years ago. He still seeks the love and attention
of His children – and especially our time.

Dear Lord Jesus, all the things that keep me
so busy will pass away. Only You will remain forever.
You are the same forever and ever. Help me not
to be so busy that I forget about You. Amen.

In the Valley of Darkness

"Blessed are those who believe without seeing Me." John 20:29

Gohan lived in a small town deep in the mountains. All he knew was the dark ravines surrounding their valley. Every morning he saw the sun rise on the one side of the valley. In the evenings he watched it set behind the mountaintops on the other side. Gohan's biggest wish was to see what it looked like on the other side of the deep, dark valley.

Uncle Kai knew all the mountain trails. He told the children about the wide open world on the other side of the mountain. And about the horizon that stretches across the end of the earth like one long straight line.

"There are no mountains that block out the horizon," Uncle Kai told them. He promised Gohan that he could go with him to see it one day.

Eventually the big day arrived. Uncle Kai and Gohan started climbing the mountain early in the morning, and in the evening they slept on a big rocky slope.

Gohan's heart was racing. *When I see it for myself, I will believe it,* he said to himself. *How is it possible that there is a flat world behind the mountains?*

Lord Jesus, please help me to believe,
even if I can't see You with my eyes. Amen.

Is it absolutely necessary to see
something before we believe it?
Read on to find the answer.

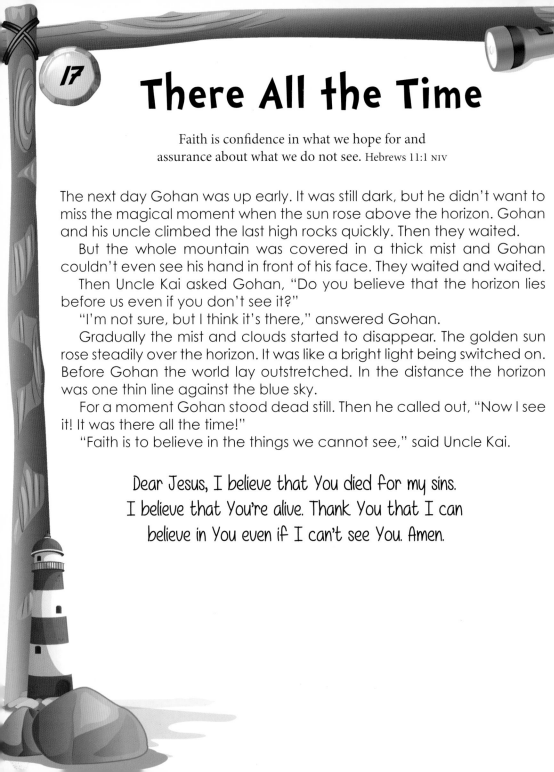

There All the Time

Faith is confidence in what we hope for and
assurance about what we do not see. Hebrews 11:1 NIV

The next day Gohan was up early. It was still dark, but he didn't want to miss the magical moment when the sun rose above the horizon. Gohan and his uncle climbed the last high rocks quickly. Then they waited.

But the whole mountain was covered in a thick mist and Gohan couldn't even see his hand in front of his face. They waited and waited.

Then Uncle Kai asked Gohan, "Do you believe that the horizon lies before us even if you don't see it?"

"I'm not sure, but I think it's there," answered Gohan.

Gradually the mist and clouds started to disappear. The golden sun rose steadily over the horizon. It was like a bright light being switched on. Before Gohan the world lay outstretched. In the distance the horizon was one thin line against the blue sky.

For a moment Gohan stood dead still. Then he called out, "Now I see it! It was there all the time!"

"Faith is to believe in the things we cannot see," said Uncle Kai.

Dear Jesus, I believe that You died for my sins.
I believe that You're alive. Thank You that I can
believe in You even if I can't see You. Amen.

The Dream Box

Everything we have has come from You, and we
give You only what You first gave us! 1 Chronicles 29:14

Once there was a little girl named Elizabeth. She had a big wooden chest in her bedroom. The chest was locked with a big lock and no one ever saw her open the chest. Her friends wondered what treasures she kept in her box.

One day her friend Annie visited. Annie wanted to see what Elizabeth kept in the chest. "Why do you keep the wooden box locked, Lizzy?" asked Annie.

"I keep my most precious possessions in there," answered Elizabeth. "Wow! That sounds wonderful! Could I see them?"

Elizabeth took the key from her bedside table drawer and unlocked the box. Annie peered inside. She couldn't believe her eyes. Her mouth fell open ... "The box is empty!" she called out.

"No, it's not. It's filled with dreams. When I dream about something that I want to do some day, then I keep it in my dream box."

"But what does that help you? You can't even see your dream!"

"I don't have to see my dreams to know they are there. I know each dream. When the time is right, I'll take one dream out and use it."

"Like what?"

"I really want to sing one day. And now I'm part of the school choir! I can praise Jesus with my voice!"

"I think I also want a dream box," said Annie, "a dream box for Jesus."

Dear Jesus, I give all my dreams to You.
I want to serve You with the talents You have given me.
Amen.

What do you keep in your dream box?

The Fishing Boat

Dear children, let's not merely say that we love each other; let us show the truth by our actions. 1 John 3:18

A ship is not built to stay in the harbor. No, a ship has a certain task to perform. Some ships are large, heavy battleships with cannons and ammunition. Other ships are designed to transport passengers. They have big dining halls, restaurants and swimming pools on the deck. There are also motor boats and sailing boats and small fishing boats. Each one is designed for a specific purpose.

Children are also like fishing boats. The Lord doesn't want you to stay anchored in the safety of the harbor. Then you are not living your true purpose. You will rust and your paint will peel off.

The Lord asks that you pull up your anchor and put your oars in the water. He knows the size of your boat and how rough the deep waters will be. Therefore He won't ask things of you that you cannot do. Best of all is that He climbs into the boat with you. The adventure with Him can begin!

Move out of the safe harbor. Row to the open seas and rough waves. Exercise your faith muscles. "But how?" you ask.

Be friendly to your classmates. Sit with the new kid in school. Give others a turn. Be nice when someone says bad things about you. God, who helps you row, will show you how.

Dear Jesus, teach me to live like a child of Yours. I don't want to just stay in the safe harbor. Thank You for getting into the boat of life with me. Amen.

How can you sail out of the safe harbor tomorrow?

You Can Make a Difference

Don't let anyone think less of you because you are young.
Be an example to all believers in what you say, in the way you
live, in your love, your faith, and your purity. 1 Timothy 4:12

In 1979 an American woman named Jamie Lash asked God to show her how she could serve and glorify Him. While she was sitting on the beach near her home, she noticed round shiny white shells. The shells were called *lucina*, which means "light."

Jamie collected the shells, drew a picture on them and wrote a Scripture verse or quote. She included her telephone number and then threw the shells back into the sea.

Jamie prayed that people who really wanted to hear about Jesus' love would pick up the shells. That's exactly what happened. Within a month people started calling her after they'd picked up the shells that had washed onto the beach.

This is how Jamie's sea shell ministry started. Thousands of people have been touched by this simple idea of writing a Scripture verse on a sea shell.

Even if we are small and can't do much, we can be obedient to God and show His love to other people, just like Jamie. You are not too small to make a difference.

Dear Lord, thank You that I
have a job to do in Your kingdom,
no matter how small I am. Help me
to show others Your love. Amen.

Salt in the Lake

Do everything without complaining and arguing, so that
no one can criticize you. Live clean, innocent lives as
children of God, shining like bright lights. Philippians 2:14-15

Long ago there was a young man who lived with his master close to a big lake. The old man taught the trainee to make boats from big tree stumps.

One day the gray-haired teacher sent him to fetch salt. The master told him to pour a handful of salt in a glass of water and then drink it.

"How does it taste?" asked the old man.

"Terribly salty!" said the unhappy young man.

Then the old man told him to throw a handful of salt in the lake and to drink a glass of that water.

"And what does it taste like?" asked the master again.

"Fresh," answered the young man, "I didn't taste the salt at all."

The wise old man explained to his student that difficulty in life is like a handful of salt. The bitterness of the situation depends on whether you throw your troubles into a glass or into a lake.

When your pain is all you see, you're the glass. You forget about all the good things in your life. But if you realize that there are many other things to be thankful for, you are more like a lake.

Only you can decide what you're going to be: a glass or a lake?

Dear Father, help me not to be like a glass of salt
water that only sees my own small issues. I want
to be a great lake of fresh water. Amen.

Wake Up Again

The LORD doesn't see things the way you see them. People judge
by outward appearance, but the LORD looks at the heart. 1 Samuel 16:7

The pyramids in Egypt were built more than five thousand years ago.
They were used as tombs to bury their pharaohs (kings). Before the
pharaohs were buried they were embalmed.

First they washed the body and then treated it with all kinds of oils
so that it did not waste away. An embalmed pharaoh was wrapped in
pieces of cloth. The face was covered with a mask on which beautiful
patterns had been painted. They also used gold and other precious
stones to decorate the body and the tomb.

However, none of these things could make the pharaoh come alive
again. The mighty ruler was dead.

When we say that we serve Jesus, but we don't live like He expects
from us, then we are like a mummy. We are beautiful on the outside,
but inside we are dead. Others can't see His power in us. The flame of
Jesus' love has died and we have become like embalmed pharaohs.

Fortunately, Jesus can wake us up and let our flame burn brightly
again.

O Lord, I'm so sorry that I'm like a mummy sometimes.
It looks like I'm a Christian, because I talk about You, but
I don't do anything for You. Wake me up again, please! Amen.

Cast Away

I am the least of all the apostles. In fact, I'm not even
worthy to be called an apostle. 1 Corinthians 15:9

Paul, one of the best-known apostles, preached everywhere and told many people about Jesus. He didn't think he was worth anything, but still the Lord used him mightily.

When a big ship sinks, some of the ship's cargo ends up in the sea. Pieces of wooden furniture float around in the waves. We call these pieces driftwood. Later they become bleached and dry from the sun and salt water.

Maybe you also feel like a piece of driftwood at times – as if you're not worth much. Maybe you didn't get chosen for the football team, or you were disappointed by your grades.

Someone once gave me a cross that they had made from driftwood. This cross reminds me that Jesus was cast away like a piece of this wood. His own people rejected Him. They nailed Him to a cross, and there He died. But He rose from the dead and now He is sitting on His throne in heaven!

Even if you sometimes feel like you're worth nothing, you must never forget that you're a child of the King. Lift up your head and live like one!

Lord Jesus, thank You for dying on the cross
to show me how much You love me. I know
I'm worth a lot to You. Amen.

Invisible Letters

Clearly, you are a letter from Christ showing the result of our ministry among you. This "letter" is written not with pen and ink, but with the Spirit of the living God. It is carved not on tablets of stone, but on human hearts. 2 Corinthians 3:3

Did you know that you can write on a piece of paper with invisible letters? It's a nifty plan if you want to write a secret letter to someone. Cut open a lemon and squeeze out the juice. Now take a paint brush and dip it in the lemon juice. Write a message to your friend on a piece of paper. Make sure that you write only friendly letters!

As the lemon juice gets dry, the words on the page will slowly disappear. No one will even guess that there is something written on the paper.

When your friend gets the letter she must ask her Mom to light a candle for her. Then she must hold the letter above the flame, but far enough so that it doesn't catch fire.

Before her eyes the letters will change color, first into a light brown color and then dark brown. She must wait patiently. It's so exciting! It will almost feel as if you are talking to her face to face.

The Bible says that we are like a letter to people. This letter is written by Christ Himself – not with ink, but on our hearts. We must therefore live so that everyone can see Christ in us.

Thank You, Lord Jesus, that I can
be a letter. May others see You when
they "read" the letter of my life. Amen.

Write a letter to Jesus and
keep it in your Bible.

25

The Chinese Vase

"In the same way, let your good deeds shine out for all to see,
so that everyone will praise your heavenly Father." Matthew 5:16

Jason was touring China and wanted to buy a special gift to take home to his mother. He bought her the most beautiful vase with Chinese patterns on it. He wrapped it carefully and put it in a sturdy box. On the box he wrote: "FRAGILE. HANDLE WITH CARE."

When he arrived home Jason couldn't wait to give the vase to his mom. He opened the box and unwrapped it. He couldn't believe his eyes! The vase was broken into many pieces.

His mom comforted him. "Don't worry, we will glue the vase back together piece by piece." The next day they bought glue and started fitting the shattered pieces into the right places. By the afternoon they were finished. The enormous vase stood upright.

"Oh no, look at all the cracks. It looks terrible," Jason said sadly. "Just wait until evening," his mom replied. When his mom called him for dinner that night, Jason walked into the dining room, which was dimly lit. In the corner stood the big vase on a little table. It looked like the vase was glowing from the inside.

His mom had put a candle inside the vase. The light shone bright through the little cracks. The whole vase was one bright light!

Dear Lord Jesus, You ask me
to shine my little light in the world.
Please help me to do this. Amen.

Jesus said: "I am the light of
the world." Find John 8:12 and
underline it in your Bible.

Even When No One Is Watching

Nothing in all creation is hidden from God. Everything is naked and exposed before His eyes, and He is the one to whom we are accountable. Hebrews 4:13

In the newspaper recently there was an article about a young man who worked as a security guard at a shopping mall. One morning he saw a shopping bag that had been left in a shopping trolley. In the bag were things that someone had bought. With it the guard also found a mobile phone and a large amount of money.

The man immediately dialed the last number on the phone. The brother of the mobile phone's owner answered and the security guard told him what had happened. The man couldn't believe his ears when he heard that the shopping bag and money were safe. He thanked the guard profusely, who was later given a reward.

But that's not the end of the story. A radio station heard about the security guard's honesty and broadcast the story. The owner of a big security company contacted the radio station and offered the man a job. Instead of meager tips each day, the man now receives a monthly salary.

Who would have thought that one small act of honesty could have such a remarkable outcome? The security guard said, "My mom taught me to always be honest. It doesn't matter if no one sees."

Dear Lord Jesus, sometimes it's hard to be honest. It's so easy to take something that does not belong to me, especially when no one is watching. Help me to never forget that You see everything. Amen.

27

Like a Wild Fire

Our tongues are small too, and yet they brag about big things.
It takes only a spark to start a forest fire! James 3:5 CEV

Can you imagine a life without fire? In wintertime we sit cozily in front of the fire. When we go camping we sing songs around the campfire. We also know that a small spark can light up a whole forest.

A few years ago my family and I saw a mountain fire break out. First it was just a small red line on the peak of the mountain. But then the wind started to blow. It looked like the wind was chasing the fire! Before we knew it, the whole mountain was covered in flames. All of this happened because one man made a small fire on the mountain without thinking.

In the Bible, James tells us that the tongue is like fire. It's a small part of our bodies, but it has great power! And, just like a fire, it can cause destruction. We must therefore think before we speak. Our words can cause a lot of heartache, or they can encourage others.

Always ask yourself three questions before you say something about someone else: Is it true? Is it friendly? Is it necessary? If you can answer yes to all three questions, you are free to tell your story.

Dear Jesus, I don't want to cause great forest fires with
my words. Help me to think before I speak. Amen.

The Bonsai Tree

Continue to follow Him. Let your roots grow
down into Him, and let your lives be built on him. Then your
faith will grow strong in the truth you were taught. Colossians 2:6-7

I recently watched someone at a nursery cut the roots of a bonsai tree.
He then planted the tree in a shallow pot and gave it some water. It was
a white stinkwood tree. When these trees grow in nature they become
very big, but because its roots were cut, the tree couldn't grow tall. For
the rest of its life it will stay a miniature tree.

The Lord's children are sometimes also like bonsai trees: They don't
grow as big as they are supposed to. Their roots are shallow and small,
and their branches remain stunted. They are nice to look at, but don't
provide branches to climb, or shelter for birds and animals.

The apostle Paul said that some of God's children are content to just
say that they know God. They don't want to learn more of Him or grow
closer to Him. They are like bonsai trees – they will never grow big and
strong.

We mustn't just think it's enough to acknowledge that Jesus died for
our sins. We must move closer to Him every day by reading the Bible
and talking to Him. And we must live in such a way that others can see
our love for the Lord.

Don't become a bonsai – grow strong and tall!

Lord, You want me to grow in faith. Help me
not to settle for being a small tree. Amen.

Listen!

My children, listen when your father corrects you.
Pay attention and learn good judgment, for I am giving you
good guidance. Don't turn away from my instructions. Proverbs 4:1-2

Listen … this is one of the words used most when God speaks to His children in the Bible. In Isaiah 55:3 we read: "Come to Me with your ears wide open. Listen, and you will find life."

To listen means to be obedient. You first have to listen and then act. Has your mother ever said to you, "Don't you have ears?"

When Jesus was on earth, He preached the same things over and over, but the people often didn't listen. One day He asked them: "You have ears – can't you hear?" (Mark 8:18).

When our ears are open to what we can learn from the Bible, then we start to understand what Jesus is saying to us. We start to really listen. And then we start to do.

Lord Jesus, everywhere in the Bible
You give us advice on how to listen and
how to make good choices. Help me
to listen and be obedient. Amen.

Read on to find out about a
different kind of "listening"
that the Bible talks about.

Talk Less, Listen More

The heavens proclaim the glory of God. The skies display His craftsmanship. They speak without a sound or word; their voice is never heard. Yet their message has gone throughout the earth, and their words to all the world. Psalm 19:1, 3-4

Often we talk too much. Sometimes it's better to keep our mouths closed! When we keep quiet, we can listen better. Take time to listen to all the noises you can hear at night: a cricket, a mosquito, the traffic driving by your house. Can you hear an ambulance, or a dog barking?

Very few people really listen to what others say. Most people prefer to talk than to listen. We see this at school – often all the children talk all at once in the classroom while the poor teacher is trying to say something.

When we become quiet, we can also hear what God wants to say to us. It's not always easy – we must learn to listen carefully before we hear His voice.

We hear God's voice in nature. When the leaves rustle in the wind, it talks about God's omnipotence. He is the only One who can make trees grow and the wind blow.

Father and Creator, thank You for creation that shows me Your greatness. Help me to listen to Your voice. Help me to understand how big You are and how small I am. Then I will know when to keep quiet and listen for Your voice. Amen.

Hear the Bells Ringing!

How beautiful on the mountains are the feet of the messenger
who brings good news, the good news of peace and salvation,
the news that the God of Israel reigns! Isaiah 52:7

There is a whole variety of bells out there. In the Swiss Alps the goat that walks in front of the herd wears a big bell around his neck so that the other goats can follow him.

The school bell tells us when school starts or when it is break time. The best sound is when the bell sounds at the end of the school day!

Church bells can be heard from far away. In cities all over the world, bells ring out every day. On Sundays the church bells invite people to come to God's house.

In the Bible we read about the bells on Aaron's robe, and how they tinkled when he entered the temple (see Exodus 28:33-35).

Other people should see that we serve God. We must be bells for Jesus. We must invite others to serve and love Him. When others see us, they should never have to wonder whether we know Him. Even if we are small, we can make a joyful noise to the Lord.

Our bells must say, "I love Jesus!" or "Come to Him!" or "Hear the good news!"

We must be like the messenger that Isaiah wrote about: "How beautiful on the mountains are the feet of the messenger who brings good news."

Thank You, Lord, that I can be
a little bell in Your kingdom. Help me
to sound the bell for Jesus. Amen.

The Sooner, the Better

Jesus gave His life to free us from every kind of sin, to cleanse us, and to make us His very own people, totally committed to doing good deeds. Titus 2:14

Linda and Jane are helping Mom to bake cookies. They are laughing and having fun around the big kitchen table. Mom gives each of the girls a piece of dough to roll out.

"Your piece is bigger than mine!" says Linda, and grabs Jane's dough. Jane gets upset and grabs her piece back. The morning that started out so well has turned sour.

"Come on, you two," says Mom, "apologize to each other. Then we can carry on baking."

"I won't apologize!" says Jane. "I didn't start it! It's all Linda's fault."

"You get angry too quickly," mumbles Linda, annoyed. "I won't say sorry. You're a real moper."

"Linda!" Mom scolds. Jane is sad because her sister called her a moper, but she feels ashamed because she became angry so quickly. "I'm sorry, Linda." Linda also feels sorry, but she still doesn't feel like apologizing. She's sulking.

"The sooner you say sorry, the easier it is to say it. If you wait too long, later you'll be too shy to apologize. Then a little piece of dough becomes a whole bowl full of dough," says Mom.

"Sorry, Mommy," says Linda shyly. And then all three start laughing.

Dear Jesus, I'm sorry for the times that I spoiled something fun by not wanting to say sorry. Help me to quickly say I'm sorry when I've done something wrong. Amen.

The Small Stuff

"The master was full of praise. 'Well done, my good and faithful servant. You have been faithful in handling this small amount, so now I will give you many more responsibilities.'" Matthew 25:21

One day the owner of a large factory appointed a young employee. His job was to keep the tools clean and in their place. He had to make sure the tools were put away neatly and the machines were clean so that the other employees could do their jobs. He was to work for a whole week first so that the owner could see if he was doing a good job.

On the first morning the owner decided to test the young man. In the farthest corner of the factory he spilled dirty water and threw garbage on the floor.

The new employee came in, put on his overall and packed the tools neatly away. He checked the machines to see if they were clean. His work was done. Then he saw the dirty floor. Even though it was not his job, he cleaned up the mess right away.

The owner, watching from his office, was pleased. Instead of waiting a week before appointing him, he walked over to the man, shook his hand and said, "When someone is faithful in the small things – even if no one sees them – they will be trustworthy with the important tasks."

Dear heavenly Father, I also want to do
my job diligently. Sometimes I'm a little lazy.
Then I only pretend to work. Please forgive me.
Help me to do more than what is expected of
me, even when no one is looking. Amen.

Give Your Best

"Be perfect, therefore, as your heavenly Father is perfect."
Matthew 5:48 NIV

I'm sure you know how difficult it is to do something perfectly, even if you try your hardest. However, we know that no one is perfect – only God.

What do you think the Bible wants to say in today's Scripture verse: "You are to be perfect"?

One day I watched a little girl of about three peering from behind her mother's dress while a lady was visiting them. She said nothing the whole time. When the woman got up to leave, the little girl jumped up and disappeared outside. She returned with flowers for the lady. They weren't very pretty flowers – just wildflowers that she'd picked outside – but the little girl gave them to the woman with a big smile. This was her very best, given with love and her whole heart.

When you give like this, in God's eyes it is perfect. He wants you to give your best. It needn't cost money. It needn't even be a real gift. It can be kind words, or friendship or love. It's not about *what* you're giving, but *how* you give.

The best you can give is yourself, just the way you are – faults and all. That's what the Lord wants from you.

Father, help me to love others like
You love me. I want to love You
with my whole heart. Amen.

Praise Him!

He holds in His hands the depths of the earth and the mightiest mountains. The sea belongs to Him, for He made it. His hands formed the dry land, too. Come, let us worship and bow down. Let us kneel before the LORD our Maker. Psalm 95:4-6

I woke up recently with the song of birds in the tree outside my bedroom window, not from an alarm clock or mobile phone. I lay in my bed and thought: *We've invented watches. It's us humans who have decided that there should be hours, days, weeks, months and years. We've decided that a hundred years is a century.*

In truth, God is the One who quietly turns spring into summer. He tells the swallows when to move to warmer places in autumn. He makes rain and snow and thunder. He created the lizards and bugs that scurry around on the ground.

Humans can't make the earth revolve around its axis and turn darkness into light. Only God can. He is omnipotent and amazing and wonderful. We should thank Him every morning for creating a brand-new day.

Lord, You are the Creator of the earth, sea, sky and all living things. Give me a thankful heart for everything that You've made. There is none like You. Amen.

Look for small things outside in nature that God created and thank Him for each one.

I Forgive You

36

"If you forgive those who sin against you, your heavenly Father will forgive you." Matthew 6:14

Hanna had a beautiful parrot. His feathers were red and yellow and shiny blue. Hanna's best friend, Ella, wanted one of the bright tail feathers. Hanna promised to give her one as soon as the parrot lost one.

One morning a long feather lay at the bottom of the cage. Hanna excitedly put the feather between the pages of one of her school books. Before school she waited for Ella.

"Look what I have for you!" Hanna said. She took out the beautiful feather and gave it to her friend. Ella jumped up and down with joy.

After the first class Ella walked to the teacher's desk and gave her something. Hanna saw how the teacher smiled and Ella walked proudly back to her chair.

Then the teacher said: "Children, look what Ella has given me." She held the feather in the air. "She brought it from home especially for me." Hanna couldn't believe her ears. She felt angry and sad at the same time.

That night Hanna told the whole story to her mother. Then her mom took the Bible and read Matthew 6:15: "If you refuse to forgive others, your Father will not forgive your sins."

Hanna didn't feel like forgiving Ella, but she knew it was the right thing to do. She prayed this prayer that night:

Dear Jesus, You know that I feel sad. I don't feel like forgiving Ella. Please help me to forgive her. Amen.

Do you think Hanna should tell Ella that she feels hurt about what she did?

Footprints

Jesus said, "I am leaving you with a gift – peace of mind and heart."
John 14:27

On one holiday our family went camping. Every morning the ranger showed us fresh tracks in the soil, some quite close to camp. There were lion tracks and cheetah tracks and also the deep round tracks of an elephant. Then there were smaller field animal prints: antelope, baboon, jackal. Each had its own unique footprint.

Wherever we go in life, we leave our footprints behind. When we are friendly towards adults and our friends, we leave footprints of love. Then people remember how well we treated them.

If we're always dissatisfied about everything, then people remember how unhappy we made them feel.

When we gossip and say bad things about others, then people see the nasty footprints we leave behind. Those footprints are without love – they walk over other people's feelings.

Jesus also left footprints behind after He ascended to heaven. He left us His peace. He wants us to follow in His steps and share His peace and love with others.

Dear Jesus, thank You for Your footprints of love
and peace all over the earth. Help me to follow in
Your steps. Then others can see Your peace in
the footprints I leave behind. Amen.

Scary Stuff

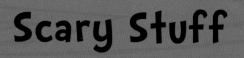

All along the path we travel we come across things that scare us.

Children are quick to say, "I can't do it!" They don't want to try because they may be afraid that others will laugh at them.

Doing bad things is another scary thing! It's like a thorn bush that scratches and stings, and holds you back so that you can't move forward.

You don't have to be afraid. God is with you. He holds your hand. Lift up your head and walk with Him!

"I hold you by your right hand – I, the LORD your God. And I say to you, 'Don't be afraid. I am here to help you.'"

Isaiah 41:13

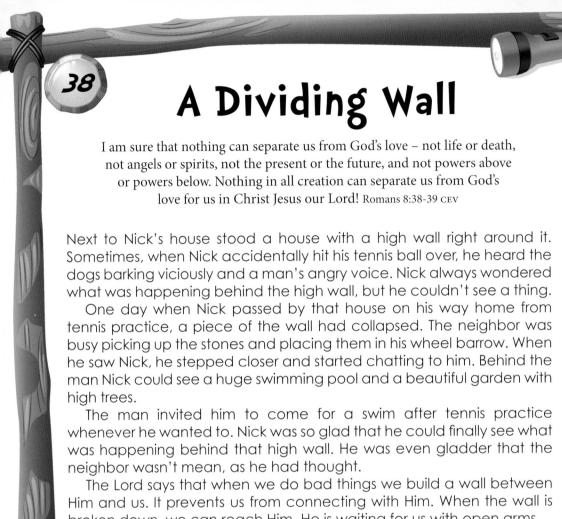

A Dividing Wall

I am sure that nothing can separate us from God's love – not life or death, not angels or spirits, not the present or the future, and not powers above or powers below. Nothing in all creation can separate us from God's love for us in Christ Jesus our Lord! Romans 8:38-39 CEV

Next to Nick's house stood a house with a high wall right around it. Sometimes, when Nick accidentally hit his tennis ball over, he heard the dogs barking viciously and a man's angry voice. Nick always wondered what was happening behind the high wall, but he couldn't see a thing.

One day when Nick passed by that house on his way home from tennis practice, a piece of the wall had collapsed. The neighbor was busy picking up the stones and placing them in his wheel barrow. When he saw Nick, he stepped closer and started chatting to him. Behind the man Nick could see a huge swimming pool and a beautiful garden with high trees.

The man invited him to come for a swim after tennis practice whenever he wanted to. Nick was so glad that he could finally see what was happening behind that high wall. He was even gladder that the neighbor wasn't mean, as he had thought.

The Lord says that when we do bad things we build a wall between Him and us. It prevents us from connecting with Him. When the wall is broken down, we can reach Him. He is waiting for us with open arms.

Thank You, Lord, for inviting me to get to be Your friend.
Please break down the wall of sin between us. Amen.

Honesty Is Best

Do not lie to each other … As God's chosen people, holy and dearly loved, clothe yourselves with compassion, kindness, humility, gentleness and patience. Bear with each other and forgive one another. Colossians 3:9, 12-13 NIV

Stephen went to school whistling a happy tune – yesterday he had found out that he had been chosen as captain of the football team! Nothing else mattered today.

When they entered Math class, Stephen greeted his strict teacher in a friendly manner – not like on other days. When they took their seats Mr. Smith asked them to take out their homework. The teacher started doing his rounds. Stephen's heart dropped.

Oh no! He hadn't done his homework. He had to think of a very good excuse.

"Stephen, where is your homework?"

"Sir," Stephen started, "I left my book at my grandma's house where I did it yesterday." Stephen felt relieved. That was easy.

"Oh, okay. Your grandmother lives close to me. I'll get your book from her when I go home this afternoon," said Mr. Smith.

"Um, my grandma is in hospital at the moment, sir," Stephen lied again.

"Shame, she must have gotten sick very quickly since yesterday," said Mr. Smith.

"Yes, it was a bit sudden, sir."

All the cheerfulness of the morning was gone. Stephen could see that Mr. Smith did not believe him. And what must his classmates think? How could he lie like that? Three times in a row!

Stephen realized it was far worse to lie and lose the respect of others than to be honest and accept your punishment.

Lord Jesus, help me not to say yes to sin. Amen.

Do you think it's right to tell a lie sometimes?

The Rocks We Carry

Jesus said, "If you are tired from carrying heavy burdens, come to Me and I will give you rest." Matthew 11:28 CEV

A group of students went mountain climbing one weekend. The route to the top of the mountain was very steep and every now and then they had to stop and help each other up.

One of the students wanted to play a trick on his friend Tom. When they stopped to rest at a stream, he put a rock in Tom's backpack. Tom couldn't understand why the last stretch was so tough. The trickster, who walked behind Tom, couldn't stop laughing.

Then suddenly it started to rain. Everybody took shelter under the nearest cliff and took out their raincoats. It was then that Tom discovered the rock in his bag.

"To think that I've struggled the whole way unnecessarily because I was carrying a heavy rock! Without this rock I could've reached the top by now!" His friend felt bad and apologized. Tom just laughed.

Often we carry heavy burdens with us – like feeling guilty when you've done something bad. Maybe you don't want to tell your mom that it was you who accidentally broke the window. Or maybe you don't want to apologize to your friend for being mean. The longer you wait, the heavier the rock becomes.

Ask Jesus to forgive you. He came to earth to help us take the rocks out of our bags one by one.

Lord Jesus, thank You for being
willing to take my heavy rocks. Amen.

The House with the Golden Windows

Be satisfied with what you have. The Lord has promised that He will not leave us or desert us. Hebrews 13:5 CEV

There once lived a boy at the edge of a small town. They had an ordinary house – it was not fancy, but also not unattractive. During the summer holiday, the boy got bored. He started finding fault with everything: His sister moaned too much; his mom gave him too many chores.

One morning while he was strolling outside, something caught his eye. Half-hidden among the tall trees on the hill near their village, he saw a house. It looked like the windows were made of gold.

What a beautiful house! he thought. *There must be fun things to do there* … He slipped out the door and off he went.

The whole time his eyes were on the golden windows. His heart raced as he climbed the rocky mountain path. His eyes were fixed on the house above him.

Finally he reached the house, but to his horror it was old and dilapidated. It was the sun's golden rays shining on the broken windows that made it look like gold. He couldn't believe it. Disappointed, he turned around and stood looking down on the town below. His eyes searched for his parents' home … and there it was. In the afternoon sun the windows were also shining bright!

Lord Jesus, help me to be happy with what I have. Help me not to think that other people's stuff is always better than mine. Thank You for everything You give me. Amen.

Feathers in the Wind

Don't use foul or abusive language. Let everything you say be good and helpful, so that your words will be an encouragement to those who hear them. Ephesians 4:29

There once was a shopkeeper who lived in a small town. Many people visited his shop and told him stories. The shopkeeper retold some of the stories. Sometimes he added his own ideas to the stories to make them sound better. Of course the people then told those stories to others. Each person told their own version of the story.

One day the shopkeeper heard about a dairy farmer who cheated someone out of money. The shopkeeper told the people who came to his shop. Not long after, the dairy farmer went bankrupt. Nobody wanted to buy his milk after what they had heard about him – even if they didn't know it was true.

The dairy farmer went to his pastor and told him what had happened. The pastor decided to call the shopkeeper and talk to him. He told him to bring a feather pillow. The pastor said to him, "You have really hurt someone because of your gossiping." The shopkeeper felt sorry. "What can I do to make up for what I have done?"

"Cut open the feather pillow and shake it out the window," the minister told him. "Now go and pick up every feather and bring them back to me."

But it was impossible. The wind had blown the feathers all over. The pastor told the shopkeeper, "In the same way, you can never take back your words."

Dear Jesus, sometimes I say ugly things about other people. Please forgive me and help me not to do this anymore. Amen.

Bad Language

Now is the time to get rid of anger, rage, malicious
behavior, slander, and dirty language. Colossians 3:8

A group of cousins was on holiday together. Among them was Nina, a shy little girl. She hadn't seen her cousins in a while and felt a bit out of place.

Nina's eldest cousin, Ben, was a real joker. Everybody liked him because he always told jokes and wrestled with the younger kids. He was everyone's hero.

Then Ben saw that Nina was sitting alone and started making silly faces. Not long after, Nina was laughing with the rest. She felt more at home. But … there was one problem. Ben swore a lot.

Everybody laughed when Ben used bad language. The younger cousins mimicked him to get his attention. When Ben said a bad word, the others would say the same thing, and then everyone would laugh.

Nina felt sad. She couldn't understand why someone would have to use bad language to be funny. She wished that she could tell Ben that he was a very nice boy without having to swear.

I'll rather keep quiet than use bad language, Nina decided.

Lord Jesus, help me not to use bad language.
I want You to always feel welcome in my company
and I know You hear every word I say. Amen.

What do you think Jesus would have done if Ben was His cousin? Would He have felt welcome in his company?

What Holds You Back?

Now you are free from the power of sin and have become slaves of God.
Romans 6:22

Robert and his dad were driving to the farm. His dad was in a hurry. They still had to feed the cattle before dark. But the pickup was going slowly.

"I wonder what's wrong with the truck. I really hope nothing is broken. It just doesn't want to come to full speed!" said Robert's dad when they reached the open road.

Suddenly Robert saw what the problem was. "Dad, the handbrake is still up!" Goodness! That's what was holding them back.

Sometimes there is something in our lives that holds us back so that we can't live life to the full. It's like a handbrake that is on when we are driving.

It could be something that makes us sad, or something that bothers us. It might be something that we've done wrong that we can't get off our minds.

When we do bad things, this prevents us from living a joyful life. It holds us back. When you've said something nasty about your friend behind her back and she finds out about it, you feel ashamed. Then you want to hide in the classroom all day and never go out to play. You wish the nasty words you said could just disappear.

The only thing that will work is to go to your friend and say you're sorry. Maybe she won't be friendly to you straightaway, but as time goes by, she'll see that you were really sorry and will want to be your friend again. Then everything will be good again! The handbrake is off.

Dear Lord Jesus, please keep me from doing wrong things that hold me back from living a life of joy. Amen.

The Trapdoor

Young people can live a clean life by obeying Your Word. Psalm 119:9 CEV

Have you ever heard of a trapdoor spider? This spider constructs a burrow with a cork-like trapdoor made of soil, vegetation and silk. The trapdoor fits so neatly over the hole that you don't notice it.

These spiders are usually nocturnal hunters, meaning they look for food at night. When an insect passes over the trapdoor, the spider feels the vibration and quickly ambushes the prey.

Doing bad things is like a trapdoor – you don't always see it and it's so nicely covered up when you walk passed that you don't see the danger. When you least expect it, you fall into the hole and sin pulls you down deeper and deeper.

When you invite Jesus to walk with you, He warns you about the spider's trapdoor. Listen carefully to His voice.

Lord Jesus, help me to live so close to You that I won't say yes to wrong things. Protect me from doing bad things that are like a trapdoor. Thank You that I can know that I'm safe with You and that You will help me up when I fall down. Amen.

See if you can help a friend who got caught up in sin without realizing it.

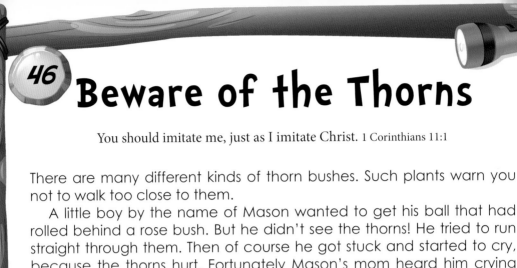

Beware of the Thorns

You should imitate me, just as I imitate Christ. 1 Corinthians 11:1

There are many different kinds of thorn bushes. Such plants warn you not to walk too close to them.

A little boy by the name of Mason wanted to get his ball that had rolled behind a rose bush. But he didn't see the thorns! He tried to run straight through them. Then of course he got stuck and started to cry, because the thorns hurt. Fortunately Mason's mom heard him crying and ran outside to find him.

While Michelle was helping her son to calm down, she said, "Don't pull. Then the thorns hook in deeper. Rather walk back the way you came in. Then you'll get unstuck faster."

That was good advice. Mason walked slowly backwards. One after the other the thorns came loose.

When we do bad things, it is like getting tangled up in thorns. We see something that we want or that looks inviting. We walk deeper and deeper into the thorn bush – until we're stuck.

Nothing can get us unstuck, except Jesus' soft voice calling us back to Him. With Him we are safe.

Jesus, thank You for calling me back to You
when I get stuck in the thorn bushes of sin.
Help me to listen to Your voice. Amen.

The Horse and the Chair

If we confess our sins to Him, He is faithful and just to forgive us our sins. 1 John 1:9

Someone sent me a picture of a horse tied to the leg of a chair. It was a plastic chair and the horse should have been able to pull the chair over and run away.

What was the horse's mistake? He thought the chair was heavy. He just had to take the first step and he would have realized that the chair could be lifted easily and pulled along.

People are often like this horse – they think they can't move because their sins are too big.

For instance, you might think about something you've done wrong and are too scared to tell anyone. Pray that God will help you to see your faults, then ask for forgiveness. You will see that it's better than to be stuck in one place with bad things in your heart.

Lord Jesus, please forgive me for the bad things
I've done. I don't want to be entangled in my sins.
Help me to take the first step away from doing
wrong things and towards You. Amen.

Always Be Thankful

As members of one body you are called to live in peace.
And always be thankful. Colossians 3:15

Sydney's mom bought her a new smartphone for her birthday. Her parents weren't very rich, so her mother had to save every month to buy this phone. She was so excited that she could buy Sydney such a super phone at a good price.

On the morning of the big day, Sydney's mom gave her the present with a big smile. She couldn't wait to see Sydney's face when she opened it.

But no! When Sydney opened the box she burst into tears. "This is *not* a nice phone. I don't want it! All my friends will laugh at me!" She ran to her room and slammed the door. Her mom was very sad. She didn't say anything and just put the phone back in its box.

Later that day Sydney went to sit with her mom in the kitchen, still sulking. Her mom explained to her that we must never think we deserve to be given a gift. Even if we don't like it, we must still be thankful that someone loved you enough to buy you a present. "The most important thing is to be thankful," she said.

Lord, please teach me to be thankful. Help me to notice how much my parents love me and all the things they do for me. Thank You for their sacrifices. Amen.

What would you have done
if you were Sydney?

Behind the Mask

"You are like whitewashed tombs – beautiful on the outside but filled
on the inside with dead people's bones and all sorts of impurity."
Matthew 23:27

Sometimes people wear masks at parties. Then you can't see who's behind the mask. You must guess. There are movie characters like Superman and Batman who also wear masks. When Superman takes off his mask, he is just an ordinary guy like everyone else.

When someone wears a mask, he or she is hiding behind it. They pretend to be someone that they're not … like Pete.

The class was quiet. The teacher asked Pete where his history assignment was. Pete answered with a sweet voice that his little brother had spilled milk all over it.

"I'm sorry, ma'am."

But when the teacher turned around, Pete pulled an ugly face at her. He is wearing a mask. He is pretending to be sorry, but behind the teacher's back he is nasty.

Jesus talked with His disciples about the same thing: He said that people who pretend to be good and do the right things to be seen by others are false. They seem clean and pure, but on the inside they are ugly.

When we pretend to serve Jesus but do wrong things when no one sees, we are wearing masks. Then we are not really God's children.

Lord Jesus, I want to be a sincere and honest child of Yours. I don't want to talk about You in church and then say and do bad things when I'm with my friends. Help me to follow You with my whole heart. Amen.

The Green-Eyed Monster

You are jealous of what others have, but you can't get it, so you fight and wage war to take it away from them. Yet you don't have what you want because you don't ask God for it. And even when you ask, you don't get it because your motives are all wrong – you want only what will give you pleasure. James 4:2, 3

Do you know what it means when someone says a person is green with envy? What do you think it could mean?

When someone else can do something better than you, you might feel jealous of that person. Maybe she is prettier than you, or has more toys. You might wish that you could swim as far, play the piano as well, or run as fast. Then you start wishing that you could be her. But because you can't be somebody else and can't do anything about all her possessions or achievements, you become jealous.

Then you start saying bad things about that person. You might even wish that he or she dies just so that you can be the best! (Wow!)

Jealousy eats you up from the inside out. You don't care what you are doing, as long as you can be the best.

The Bible gives us good advice. James says that we must pray. This doesn't mean that we must pray for the same things as the person we're jealous of. No, we must pray that God will change our hearts so that we can be happy with what we have.

Lord, please show me the special
gifts that You've given me. Help me to be
thankful for what I have received. Amen.

A Cheerful Giver

51

"Give, and it will be given to you. A good measure, pressed down, shaken together and running over, will be poured into your lap. For with the measure you use, it will be measured to you." Luke 6:38 NIV

Beth and her brother, Ted, came home from athletics practice tired and hungry. On the kitchen table two big slices of delicious cake were waiting for them.

"I knew you would like some of Grandma's birthday cake when you got home, so I brought you each a piece," said Mom.

Beth took her cake and juice. Ted sat down next to her and tucked into his slice. Soon Ted's cake was all gone! He looked hungrily at what Beth had left.

Noticing his stares, Beth laughed. "Don't worry, you can have the rest of mine. I know you're always hungry!"

Ted felt ashamed. "Thanks. I'll share my sweets with you sometime."

"You don't have to," his sister replied, "I like giving you things, Ted."

Jesus teaches us that when we give to others, we will be blessed, even if it is not right away. However, if we're always measuring things and are reluctant to share, we will not receive much in return.

It's contagious: When someone gives with a cheerful heart, others also want to give.

Lord Jesus, help me to give with open hands
and without expecting anything in return. Amen.

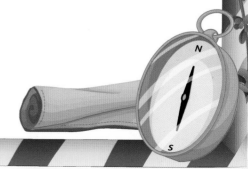

Be Appreciative

One of them (the ten lepers), when he saw he was healed, came back,
praising God in loud voice. He threw himself at Jesus' feet and thanked Him.
Luke 17:15-16 NIV

In the Bible we are told a story about a small town that was surrounded by a powerful king and his army. There was no way the citizens could escape.

The people inside the city walls were very scared that the gates would somehow be opened or that the enemy would climb over the walls and gain access.

In the small town there lived a poor but wise man. Through this man's advice the city was saved.

One would think that they would have celebrated and feasted to thank this man who saved their lives. But that's not what happened. In Ecclesiastes 9:15 we read, "But afterward no one thought to thank him."

Today, people are still eager to ask for advice and favors from others, but very few take the time to go and say thank you afterwards.

Lord, help me to notice when someone does
something for me, and to sincerely thank them.
Thank You for everything You have given me. Amen.

Is there someone that you should thank today? Do it now!

Don't Be Judgmental

Jesus said, "The standard you use in judging is
the standard by which you will be judged." Matthew 7:2

Two sisters were standing by the window admiring the flowers growing along their fence. An elderly woman was walking by, and suddenly she knelt down beside a beautiful rose. She gripped the stem as if she wanted to pick the flower.

The one sister was furious. "She wants to pick our beautiful roses! They don't belong to her! She must leave our roses alone!"

The other sister replied, "I don't think she wants to pick the rose. She just wants to touch it and smell it."

"I'm going to tell her not to pick our flowers!" When she got outside the lady looked up and smiled. "You've got such lovely roses. I don't have a garden, but I walk passed here every day to look at your flowers. Thank you!"

The sister felt ashamed. There she was, thinking the worst of an innocent lady! She had judged her without giving her a chance.

Do you sometimes do the same thing? We see a new kid in school and decide we don't like her because she keeps everyone at a distance. But maybe she's just shy. Go and talk to her. She might just become your best friend.

Lord Jesus, I often decide for myself that
someone has bad intentions or is wrong before
I give them a chance or get to know them.
Please help me not to judge people, but rather
to look for the good in them. Amen.

A Torn Picture

"Treat others as you want them to treat you." Matthew 7:12 CEV

The bell rang and the school children, feeling hot and tired, entered the class room after lunch break. Jared bumped hard into Aiden who was knocked over and in the process lost his glasses. In the corner two girls giggled while pointing at Aiden.

The teacher waited for everyone to take their seats. Then she took a big blank white paper and put it on the blackboard with two magnets. She drew a little girl with a friendly face, curly hair and a pretty flower dress.

But then she did a strange thing: She pulled the picture off the board and started talking.

"Your hair looks terrible today, Susan," she said, and tore the head off the picture. "Your dress is not as pretty as mine," and she tore the dress in half.

The children waited with bated breaths. The teacher continued until there was only a heap of pieces of paper left.

Then she said, "Who wants to glue the pieces back together?" A couple of children put up their hands and started to glue the pieces together on a new blank paper. When all the pieces was back together, the teacher put it up on the blackboard again. The girl didn't look so good – everything was lop-sided.

"This is what happens when we are rude to our friends. We tear the friend to pieces bit by bit through our words and actions. And it's not easy to put the pieces back together. Remember this next time."

She looked at Aiden and smiled at him. He grinned back.

Dear Jesus, help me to be kind to everyone. Amen.

A Stone in the Road

Some of you say, "We can do whatever we want to!" But I tell you that not everything may be good or helpful. We should think about others and not about ourselves.
1 Corinthians 10:23-24 CEV

There was once a king who wanted to test his servants. He buried a treasure right in the middle of the road leading to the city. Then he rolled a big stone over the treasure. He didn't tell anyone about the treasure and waited to see what would happen.

The people using the road were annoyed. Some of them climbed over the stone. Others tried to pass with their wagons on either side. But no one tried to move the stone out of the way.

In the late afternoon a man and his wife came traveling along the road with their horse and carriage. They were on their way home.

"Wow, look at this big stone. No one with their horse and carriage will be able to pass," said the man. "Let's tie the rock to our carriage and try to pull it out of the way."

After much effort they were able to move the stone out of the road. There – in the last rays of the sun – a heap of gold coins shimmered. "It must belong to the king," said the man's wife. Even though it was already dark, they turned around and took the money to the king.

The next day the king summoned everyone to the castle. He called the man and his wife and thanked them for their kindness. Then he gave them the whole bag of gold coins!

Dear Jesus, sometimes I only think about myself. Please help me to be considerate of others and to think of others' needs before my own. Amen.

56

Do What Is Right

*If anyone, then, knows the good they ought to
do and doesn't do it, it is sin.* James 4:17 NIV

There was a new boy in Fred's class. His name was Hank. He seemed nice, but he was very shy. Fred knew that he should invite Hank to play ball with them, but he didn't want to. What if Hank took his place on the football team? The new boy was big and it looked like he could kick the ball very far. And maybe even run very fast. So Fred kept quiet and ignored Hank.

A few weeks later one of the first team's players fell ill just before a very big match. The coach was in a panic. He called in all the boys in Fred's grade, but there seemed to be no one who could be a good replacement.

Then the coach saw the new boy. "Can you play football, Hank?"

"Yes, sir," Hank replied.

"And can you run fast?"

"They say so, sir."

And that's how Hank got a place in the first team and helped them win a very important game. Fred felt bad that he hadn't asked Hank to play with them from the start. He knew it would have been the right thing to do.

Lord, I know what is right, but I don't
always do it. Please forgive me for when
I do the wrong thing instead. Help me to
make the right choice next time. Amen.

The Sparrow

"What is the price of five sparrows – two copper coins?
Yet God does not forget a single one of them. And the very hairs
on your head are all numbered. So don't be afraid; you are more
valuable to God than a whole flock of sparrows." Luke 12:6-7

A sparrow is a very small bird. Sparrows don't have bright showy feathers, like peacocks do. Neither do they have sharp beaks like woodpeckers. They don't make their nests high up on cliffs like eagles. And they can't catch fish with their claws like a fish eagle. They can't even sing like canaries, let alone talk like a parrot!

No, a sparrow is a very ordinary little bird that eats seeds and leftover crumbs. Maybe you also sometimes feel like a sparrow: Small. Unimportant. Dull.

Maybe you wish you could do big and important things or that others would notice you. You might wish that you were pretty, or that someone would notice your voice among the many other voices at school.

In biblical times, sparrows were also unimportant little birds. Still, Jesus told the people that not one single sparrow is forgotten by God – no matter how small or unimportant. Jesus also assured the people that they are more valuable to God than a whole flock of sparrows.

You might seem ordinary to everyone else, but you are strong and brave. Jesus wants you to believe in yourself. Believe in Him – He will give you the strength to do anything.

Jesus, thank You for making me
far more valuable than a whole
flock of sparrows. Amen.

Look for a sparrow's feather.
Keep it in your Bible.

All Things Are Possible

For I can do everything through Christ, who gives me strength. Philippians 4:13

Dr Seuss is a famous author of children's books. He encourages children to believe in themselves and to see the world through different eyes.

Dr Seuss once said, "Think left and think right and think low and think high. Oh, the thinks you can think up if only you try!"

Sometimes we think ourselves into a corner. Your mom says, "Go to sleep. You've studied hard enough." But then you think, *I'm not good at Math. I'm going to fail.*

Or someone makes fun of you and says, "Look at all your freckles."

When you look at yourself in the mirror – you see only freckles. And you start to think that you're ugly!

Maybe a teacher once told you, "You're not going to get very far in life. You're struggling too much to read." And you believed it.

God wants you to believe that He made you good, and special, and beautiful. If the Lord Himself thinks so, who are you to think otherwise? He doesn't want you to think that you will fail. What He wants is for you to believe that with His help you can do anything!

Dr Seuss's poem could have gone something like this: "Think left and think right and think low and think high. Oh, the places I will go! With God's help, I will fly!"

Dear Lord, thank You that I can do all
things through Christ who gives me strength.
Help me to take this to heart. Amen.

With Jesus on Your Side

Have I not commanded you? Be strong and courageous. Do not be afraid; do not be discouraged, for the LORD your God will be with you wherever you go. Joshua 1:9 NIV

In the Cape Winelands in South Africa, you find the Swartberg Pass and the Bainskloof Pass. These passes were built by Andrew Bain, the most famous road engineer of South Africa, together with his son, Thomas.

In those early days they didn't have modern equipment to build roads that we have today. Most of the passes were built with the help of convicts and prisoners of war.

One day the mayor of Prince Albert asked Thomas Bain if he would find out if it was possible to build a road over the Swartberg in the Karoo (an inaccessible part in the south of the country). The mayor thought it might be impossible. He told Bain that his report would probably contain only one word: *Impassable*.

After a few weeks Bain was back. His words to the mayor was: "You were right. My report is short, even shorter than you thought. It contains only one word: *Passable*."

We often think that something is impossible to do. Maybe it's school work or a difficult piece of music or being able to bowl straight at the wickets. The Bible teaches us not to become discouraged. Try it one more time ...

Dear Father, You teach me to never give up. Help me to put my faith in You. Amen.

Implosion

"I am creating something new. There it is! Do you see it?" Isaiah 43:19 CEV

Are you familiar with the word *implode*? Implode is a word that you use to describe when a block of flats or a big office building is demolished.

Explosive experts – the people who know how to work with dynamite and other explosives – pack the explosives in and around the building. The streets are closed off and the traffic police ensure that no vehicles or pedestrians are standing near the building. Then the building can be demolished.

A person standing a safe distance away pushes a heavy lever that is connected to the explosives. From far away one can hear an enormous bang. Sometimes one can even feel a slight tremor. Where the building once stood, a huge cloud of dust rises. When the dust settles, only a heap of rubble remains: the building has been imploded.

Where there once stood walls and windows, only a big hole is left. Now the earthmovers can remove the rubble and then the bulldozers will level the ground. Later a brand-new building will be built in its place.

Sometimes something bad happens and it might feel like your life is imploding. It seems as though everything is collapsing around you. However, as time goes by, it *will* get better. Little by little. Just like rubble that is removed. Then the Lord does something new in your life, making things just as good, or even better than they were before.

Thank You, Lord Jesus, that You can turn the sad experiences of my life into something good. Amen.

Tidying Up

"Come to Me, all of you who are weary and carry
heavy burdens, and I will give you rest." Matthew 11:28

Jill has been looking for her pink scarf with the polkadots all afternoon. She and her friends want to go to town, and the scarf will match her new top perfectly. She pulls out all her drawers and starts to go through all her clothes.

Among her socks she sees the bracelets she's been looking for. She puts those with her other necklaces. Then among all the scattered clothes she finds the birthday card Grandma gave her, with some money inside. Great!

While she is tidying up, she finds all kinds of things she had forgotten about: sea shells; her torch; her sister's earrings that she never returned. Jill makes a pile for all the things she doesn't need or use anymore. Then she packs everything neatly back into the drawers. She turns to her shoes and tidies up the higgledy-piggledy pile. And there in the corner, she sees her pink scarf!

She feels so much better. Everything is neat and tidy in its place, and in the process she found her favorite scarf.

It is also necessary to unpack everything that's going on in our lives before Jesus, and ask Him to help us sort things out and tidy up.

Dear Lord Jesus, I want to unpack my mixed up
thoughts and worries before You, so that You can
quiet my heart and encourage me to lean on You. Amen.

Make a list of the things that
upset you. Then give them to
Jesus and tear up the paper.

A Mirror

Now we see things imperfectly, like puzzling reflections in a mirror, but then we will see everything with perfect clarity. 1 Corinthians 13:12

In biblical times they didn't have mirrors like we do today. The people used copper plates, which they hammered and polished until they shined. This is what they used as a mirror.

You can't see your face very clearly in the reflection of a copper plate – probably just the outline of your face and hair. The image would be dull and unclear.

Some things in our lives are also like dim mirrors. For instance, it's often unclear why certain things happen. An earthquake happens and thousands of people die ... pleasant things happen to bad people, while good people suffer ... parents get divorced ... your best friend doesn't want to play with you anymore ... you have a disability and can't understand why you're not normal like everyone else.

That is all part of the imperfect world in which we live. One day, however, we will be able to see clearly and distinctly why these things took place.

The only thing that we can do is to live close to the Lord. When something happens that you don't understand, pray that Jesus will hold you tight and show you what to do. Don't keep looking in a dim mirror; instead, keep your eyes on Jesus.

Lord Jesus, there are so many things I don't understand. One thing I know for sure: You will never abandon me. Thank You for this reassurance. Amen.

The Red Poppy

That's why I take pleasure in my weaknesses, and in the insults, hardships, persecutions, and troubles that I suffer for Christ. For when I am weak, then I am strong. 2 Corinthians 12:10

Do you know what a poppy flower looks like? It's a flower that mostly grows wild in the field. It's usually red, but sometimes they are yellow or pink. A poppy swaying in the wind is so beautiful.

You can buy poppy seed to sow in your garden, but they don't always look as cheerful and joyful as the wild poppies.

A friend told me that they even saw a red poppy growing near to a beach, where it is windy, sandy and barren.

Children of God are like red poppies that make the world a beautiful place.

Sometimes it might feel like you're a red poppy growing in the sand, and that your roots have to hold on for dear life. It's not so easy. But when you lift your head and turn your face toward the Lord, He will help you to stand tall. Even though the soil is shallow and barren, you can still bloom.

Lord Jesus, sometimes I feel small and insignificant.
Teach me to turn my head towards You every day,
so that I can stand tall and proud. Amen.

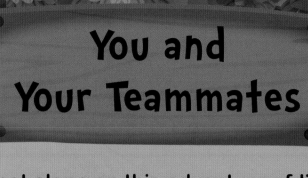

You and Your Teammates

We are not alone on this adventure of life.

We have co-hikers: our parents, brothers, sisters, family and friends, and even strangers.

Sometimes we walk along cheerfully, arm in arm. At other times we are cross and don't want anything to do with each other.

The Lord helps us to hold hands – He binds us together with chords of love.

Dear friends, let us continue to love one another, for love comes from God. Anyone who loves is a child of God and knows God.

1 John 4:7

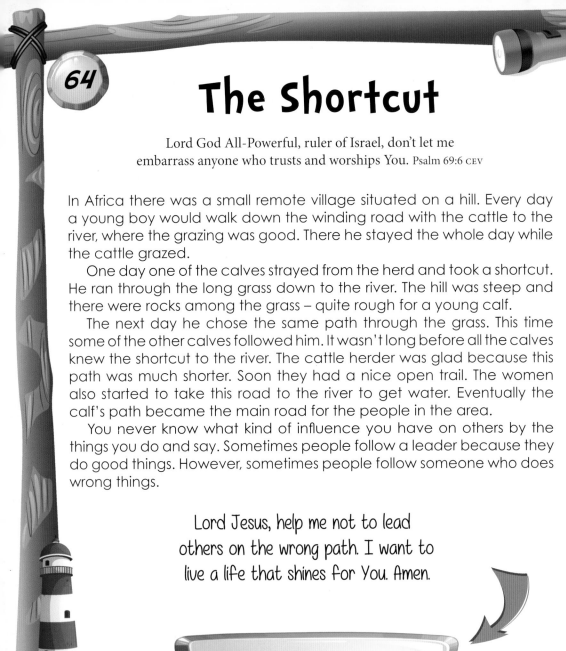

The Shortcut

Lord God All-Powerful, ruler of Israel, don't let me
embarrass anyone who trusts and worships You. Psalm 69:6 CEV

In Africa there was a small remote village situated on a hill. Every day a young boy would walk down the winding road with the cattle to the river, where the grazing was good. There he stayed the whole day while the cattle grazed.

One day one of the calves strayed from the herd and took a shortcut. He ran through the long grass down to the river. The hill was steep and there were rocks among the grass – quite rough for a young calf.

The next day he chose the same path through the grass. This time some of the other calves followed him. It wasn't long before all the calves knew the shortcut to the river. The cattle herder was glad because this path was much shorter. Soon they had a nice open trail. The women also started to take this road to the river to get water. Eventually the calf's path became the main road for the people in the area.

You never know what kind of influence you have on others by the things you do and say. Sometimes people follow a leader because they do good things. However, sometimes people follow someone who does wrong things.

Lord Jesus, help me not to lead
others on the wrong path. I want to
live a life that shines for You. Amen.

Which path are you walking on?

The Apple of His Eye

"Whoever touches you touches the apple of His eye." Zechariah 2:8 NIV

The apple of your eye is the circular inner part of your eye that enables you to see. This part of the eye is very precious, because if it gets damaged you can become blind.

Your grandmother might say to you, "You are the apple of my eye." She means that you are a precious treasure – as valuable as her eyes.

In the Bible, God called Israel the apple of His eye. Even though they were disobedient and unfaithful to Him, the Lord still loved them and took care of them. Even when they bowed before other gods, He couldn't forget them and wept over them.

Then they were exiled (sent away from their country) to Babylon. After many years, when the people were sorry for their sins, the Lord allowed them to return. He loved them very much; they were still the apple of His eye.

Similarly, you are very special to God. He is sad when you are disobedient and naughty. He wants you to love Him just as much as He loves you. You are the apple of His eye.

Thank You, Lord, that I am the apple of Your eye.
Help me to never forget this and to be obedient. Amen.

You're Special

God has given each of you a gift from His great variety of
spiritual gifts. Use them well to serve one another. 1 Peter 4:10

When you pick up a sea shell and hold it in your hand, you'll see a tiny black dot in the middle of the shell's pattern.

Scientists say that this dot holds the pattern or DNA of a specific shell. It determines from the beginning what the shell will eventually look like, even when the shell is still small.

A gray and black clamshell is always a clamshell. It cannot turn into a round white shell. Similarly, a bristly sea urchin cannot become a cowry with shiny insides. Each shell is exactly as it should be from the start, just like you.

You're special. There is only one person like you on this earth. No one else can be like you. Therefore don't try to be someone else. God made you to be *you*! You're the best you! And He has a special job especially for you to do on earth.

Dear Father, thank You for making me special.
Help me to love the person I am and not want
to be someone else. You gave me a special
job; show me what it is. Amen.

Selfies

"Those who love their life in this world will lose it. Those who care nothing for their life in this world will keep it for eternity." John 12:25

People today like to take "selfies" – photos you take of yourself. There's nothing wrong with this. However, when you start to think that you're better than others – or if other people also think you're pretty or smart or cute – then a selfie is a way to show off.

There are two ways to live your life. Take a piece of paper and draw a circle on it. Draw a chair in the middle of the circle. Now draw a stick figure sitting on the chair. This is what it looks like when a person's life revolves only around him or herself. Write: *I sit on the throne of my life*.

Now draw another circle with a chair in the middle. Now draw a cross on the chair and a crown above the cross. This is what it looks like when Christ is the center of your life. Write: *Jesus sits on the throne of my life*.

Draw one more circle with two chairs. Draw Christ's big chair in the middle and your small chair on the side. Now draw a few more chairs in the circle. Give names to each chair: Dad, Mom, your sister, your brother, friends. Also write things that you like to do around the circle, like sport, music or reading.

When Christ is the center of your life, all the other people and activities will fall into place. That's what the picture of our lives should look like.

Lord Jesus, I want You to be in charge of my life. Amen.

Keep the picture of the circles and chairs in your Bible.

Precious as a Pearl

Let us think of ways to motivate one another to acts of love and good works.
Hebrews 10:24

We all know what pearls look like. Women like to wear pearl earrings or strings of pearls around their wrist or neck. Pearls have a soft hue that almost glows.

A pearl starts to form when a very small grain of sand ends up inside the shell of an oyster. This grain of sand scratches the soft fleshy interior of the shell. The organism inside the shell secretes a substance to protect itself from the sand granule. Without anybody seeing, little by little, a precious pearl starts to form inside.

Did you know it can take up to seven years for one pearl to grow? When the pearl fishers eventually open the oyster, the most beautiful, smooth pearl is ready to be removed.

Similarly, each of us is like a precious pearl to Jesus. We must allow Him to shape and mold us so that our colors can shine.

We are all precious pearls that belong to Jesus. And when we are with other pearls, we reflect each other's dazzling colors. Together we carry the message of God's love to the world.

Lord, thank You that I'm as precious as a pearl.
Help me to remember that I need other pearls
to be able to properly glorify Your name. Amen.

When you go to sleep tonight, remind yourself that you are a precious pearl to Jesus!

Bigger and Better

You should remember the words of the Lord Jesus:
"It is more blessed to give than to receive." Acts 20:35

Riana was very excited about her birthday that was coming up. Her mom said she could invite all her friends to her party. Riana wondered what games they would play on the day. Then she thought about all the nice gifts she'd be receiving.

There was one problem: her best friend's parents didn't have money to buy an expensive gift. Riana knew that her friend would feel embarrassed to arrive without anything.

Then Riana thought of a plan. Instead of the normal birthday invitation, she wrote the following: *Come to my party on Friday. Don't bring any gifts. You are my gifts. And my party is my gift to you.* It was Riana's best birthday ever!

We live in a society where people often think only about themselves and their needs. We often hear, "I want to win. I want the latest and greatest smartphone. I must be the smartest. I want to wear the most expensive clothes. My dad has the most important job."

We seem to want things all the time. We want more and better things. When we do this, we forget what the Bible says: "Don't look out only for your own interests, but take an interest in others, too" (Philippians 2:4).

Dear Jesus, help me to remember that
it's better to give than to receive. Amen.

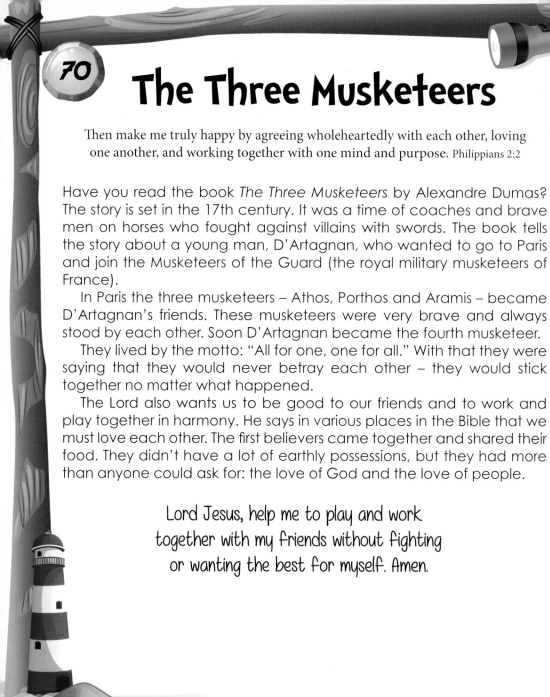

The Three Musketeers

Then make me truly happy by agreeing wholeheartedly with each other, loving one another, and working together with one mind and purpose. Philippians 2:2

Have you read the book *The Three Musketeers* by Alexandre Dumas? The story is set in the 17th century. It was a time of coaches and brave men on horses who fought against villains with swords. The book tells the story about a young man, D'Artagnan, who wanted to go to Paris and join the Musketeers of the Guard (the royal military musketeers of France).

In Paris the three musketeers – Athos, Porthos and Aramis – became D'Artagnan's friends. These musketeers were very brave and always stood by each other. Soon D'Artagnan became the fourth musketeer.

They lived by the motto: "All for one, one for all." With that they were saying that they would never betray each other – they would stick together no matter what happened.

The Lord also wants us to be good to our friends and to work and play together in harmony. He says in various places in the Bible that we must love each other. The first believers came together and shared their food. They didn't have a lot of earthly possessions, but they had more than anyone could ask for: the love of God and the love of people.

Lord Jesus, help me to play and work
together with my friends without fighting
or wanting the best for myself. Amen.

The Red Riders

*"This is My commandment: Love each other in
the same way I have loved you."* John 15:12

When I was at primary school we had a gang called the Red Riders. We built a fort in a tree with planks. There we made all kinds of secret plans.

We also had rules: We had to be kind to elderly people. We were to help each other. And no one was allowed to disclose the gang's secrets. We promised to stay true to one another.

A gang usually has a motto, which tells the members how to behave. Our motto was: "Keep your eyes on the road." The Red Riders always had to be on the lookout for people to help, almost like Robin Hood and his gang.

We also had a secret code. If you didn't know the password, you couldn't gain entry to our fort. Our secret code was: *Red Riders Rescue.*

Everyone who loves Jesus belongs to His gang. The name of His gang is *Children of Jesus* and our motto is *Love Each Other.* The secret code is the best one ever: *Jesus Loves You!*

Lord Jesus, thank You that I can belong to
Your gang. Thank You that I'm safe with You,
and for teaching me how to love others. Amen.

Read tomorrow's devotion to find
out how to write a secret letter.

The Secret Code

"There is no greater love than to lay down one's life for one's friends." John 15:13

When children belong to a gang they usually have a secret writing code and code words that only they understand and know. When other children read the letters that the gang members write to each other, they don't understand a word.

When someone picks up a note saying: G<u>y</u>d l<u>y</u>v<u>w</u>s <u>yy</u>z, they won't know what it means. But if someone knows the code for each vowel, he or she will be able to decode the words. The code looks like this: a=<u>v</u>; e=<u>w</u>; i=<u>x</u>; o=<u>y</u>; u=<u>z</u>. Now you can read what is written above.

And can you also decipher this note? Fill in the correct vowel in the place of the underlined letter.

G<u>y</u>d g<u>v</u> v <u>w</u> H<u>x</u>s <u>y</u>n<u>w</u> <u>v</u>nd <u>y</u>nl<u>y</u> S<u>y</u>n, s<u>y</u> th<u>v</u>t <u>w</u> v <u>w</u>r<u>yy</u>n<u>w</u> wh<u>y</u> b<u>wlx</u>w<u>v</u>ws <u>x</u>n H<u>x</u>m w<u>x</u>ll n<u>y</u>t p<u>w</u>r<u>x</u>sh b<u>z</u>t h<u>v</u>v<u>w</u> <u>w</u>t<u>w</u>rn<u>v</u>l l<u>x</u>f<u>w</u>.

Look up the Scripture verse in your Bible in John 3:16 to see if you got it right.

This is one of the most important Scripture verses in the Bible. It unlocks the door to heaven. It tells you about God's great love and His greatest sacrifices for each one of us, which includes you.

Now write these words in big letters on a piece of paper and write your name in the blanks: For God so loved me (your name) that He gave His one and only Son, that I (your name) who believes in Him shall not perish but have eternal life.

Learn the words off by heart so that you can say them out loud whenever you feel scared or alone.

Lord Jesus, You died on the cross for my sins, so that I can live. Thank You! Amen.

> **Learn John 3:16 off by heart so that you can recite it whenever you feel alone or scared.**

The Bright Side of Life

Being content is as good as an endless feast. Proverbs 15:15 CEV

A wise man once said that life is more fun when you look for things to laugh about.

Tina, however, always saw the negative side of everything. When her friends said, "Let's go play in the park!" she sighed and said it was too hot. Or too cold. Or the wind was blowing. Or it would be boring.

Then new neighbors moved in next door to Tina. From the first day Tina could hear someone singing and laughing cheerfully. The next day on her way to school she heard someone call out: "Hey! Wait for me!"

Tina didn't feel like waiting, but when she looked up the girl with the thick glasses was walking next to her. She talked without ever stopping!

"I live next door. Can I walk with you? My name is Nita. And yours?"

"Tina," mumbled Tina. "Wow, it almost sounds like my name. Nita and Tina!" Nita kept on talking.

"My mom enrolled me yesterday. I'm in Mr Smith's class." Mr Smith was also Tina's teacher. Before long the two girls became best friends.

The other kids couldn't believe how much Tina changed. When she was with Nita you could hear them laughing from far away. The teachers called them the cheerful twins. And almost nobody noticed that Nita was actually blind in her one eye …

Lord, help me to make the people
around me happy. Give me a cheerful
heart – even if life is hard. Amen.

Jesus' Hands and Feet

Don't get tired of helping others. You will be rewarded
when the time is right, if you don't give up. Galatians 6:9 CEV

A group of businessmen was in a hurry to get home. Their bus was late and they had to run to the airport terminal building to be on time for their flight. On their way a girl was sitting on the corner of the street selling apples. One of them knocked over her basket, and the apples scattered in all directions.

The men were so worried that they were going to miss their flight that they kept on running. One of them, however, felt sorry for the girl and stopped. He told the rest of the guys that he would take the next flight. He turned back. When he got back to where the girl was, she was on all fours trying to find the apples. Tears ran down her face. She couldn't see the apples. She was blind.

The friendly man quickly helped her to put all the apples back in the basket. Then the little girl asked, "Sir, are you Jesus?"

"No," the man laughed, "why do you ask?"

"I prayed that Jesus would help me find and pick up my apples … and then you came to help. Thank you so much!"

We are Jesus' hands and feet on earth – He works through us. When we do good things for others, they can see Him in us.

Lord Jesus, I want to be Your hands
and feet on earth. Please show me ways in
which I can show Your love to others. Amen.

Look out for ways in which
you can help others -
without being asked to.

The Concert

Above all, clothe yourselves with love, which binds
us all together in perfect harmony. Colossians 3:14

A school concert is a delightful and jolly event. It might not always be fun to practice, but on the day of the concert when you walk onto the stage, you forget about all school work and difficulties.

In your concert clothes you become a princess or a prince, or even a monkey or a big elephant. It doesn't matter what role you are playing, when you put on the costume, you become the character.

The Scripture verse for today says that we must clothe ourselves with love. It means we must "wear love." In the same way you wear the character's costume on stage and become the character, Jesus' love becomes a part of you when you wear it every day.

Love binds us together. This means that love is like a belt that you wear around your waist. Love binds all good things together and helps us to live in harmony with others.

Dear Lord Jesus, I want to wear
Your love like a beautiful robe every
day. Please help me to do this. Amen.

The Ultimate Goal

Yes, everything else is worthless when compared with the infinite value of knowing Christ Jesus my Lord. For His sake I have discarded everything else.
Philippians 3:8

Jesse Owens was an American track athlete who won four gold medals at the 1936 Olympic Games, held in Berlin. Can you imagine the practice and effort it required to achieve this! He must have been very nervous before each race. Maybe he even wondered if he had the skill and strength to cross the finish line first.

Just think what a fantastic feeling it must be to hear your name being called and then to stand on the podium while your country's national anthem is played and the flag is raised. It must have been unforgettable.

Later, however, Jesse Owens wrote, "The battles that count aren't the ones for gold medals. The struggles within yourself – the invisible, inevitable battles inside all of us – that's where it's at."

He is right. The achievements that people see don't matter in the end. If we are the best student in class or the best public speaker, it doesn't matter. The things that count most in God's eyes are those things that no one can see. He's not going to ask you one day how many medals you won. He's going to ask you if you loved Him with your whole heart and loved the people around you. He's also going to ask you if you told other people about His love. That's all that matters.

Dear Jesus, help me to love You above all things. Amen.

A Sweet Smell

He uses us to spread the knowledge of Christ
everywhere, like a sweet perfume. 2 Corinthians 2:14

Lisa's mom is busy cooking dinner in the kitchen. Lisa can smell a dessert from her room. She jumps up and runs to the kitchen.

"Mom, can I help?" Lisa asks.

"I want to make custard," she replies.

Mom is glad that Lisa wants to help. Now she can set the table. It's a special dinner because it's Lisa's grandmother's birthday and the family is coming for dinner.

Lisa knows how to make custard and pours four cups of milk into a pot. First she turns the stove on to a low heat, but when it takes a long time for the milk to boil, she turns it up. Then she remembers that she still has to wrap Grandma's gift.

I won't be long, she thinks, and runs to her room. Oh no, the gift is not where she left it! She starts looking all over for it, but the little box with the brooch is nowhere to be seen.

Then she smells something burning. She hears her mother's angry voice, "Lisa!" When she gets to the kitchen, the milk has boiled over. The delicious smell of pot roast and dessert is gone and everything smells of burnt milk.

Lisa feels bad. She wanted Grandma to walk in and smell the wonderful aromas of the food.

Her mother quickly opens all the windows and takes the burnt pot outside. Soon the other delicious smells fill the house again.

Lord Jesus, I want to be like sweet perfume.
Please help me in doing this. Amen.

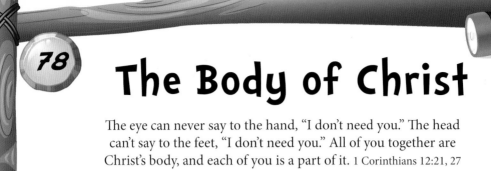

The Body of Christ

The eye can never say to the hand, "I don't need you." The head can't say to the feet, "I don't need you." All of you together are Christ's body, and each of you is a part of it. 1 Corinthians 12:21, 27

Sometimes children like to brag. One says, "I'm a better cricket player than you. I've bowled out three guys in a row." Another says, "I got a lot of trophies at the prizegiving."

Such children forget one important thing: They would not have been able to achieve anything without the help of others.

The good bowler wouldn't have been able to achieve much without good fielders. And it's not nice for an athlete to run a race without spectators!

Each one of us has a task to perform. Some of us get noticed; others stay in the background. Some children will sweep the classroom floor without being asked, while others will notice when someone is sad or lonely.

The Bible says we are one body with many parts. As today's Scripture verse tells us, "The eye can never say to the hand, 'I don't need you.' The head can't say to the feet, 'I don't need you.'"

Jesus Christ's children must work together as one body. The pastor is no more important than the little boy listening to the sermon. The one who prays is not more important than the one who helps others.

Lord Jesus, I'm just one small part of
Your body, but I know that You still need me.
I want to do my best for You. Amen.

This Is Love!

Dear friends, since God loved us that much,
we surely ought to love each other. 1 John 4:11

The apostle John was called the "apostle of love." He lived a long life and still preached every Sunday despite people having to assist him to church. Every Sunday he just preached one sentence before they carried him out again: "My dear children, you must love each other."

Later the churchgoers became tired of hearing the same thing. *All that trouble just for this!* they thought.

One day they decided to ask John about it. He answered that it was because this is what the Lord wants from us.

Sometimes it's hard to love your brother when he teases you all the time. You might be jealous of a friend because you don't have enough love in your heart. Perhaps you're lazy in reading your Bible and praying because your love for God is not as strong as it should be. Or you could be disobedient to your parents because you think only about your own interests.

I want to do this. My things are more important. If you don't have enough love in your heart, you think like this.

Jesus says to His followers that the Bible can be summed up in one sentence: Love the Lord and love others.

Now go out and do this.

Lord Jesus, help me to love others.
And to love You above all else. Amen.

How can you live a life
of love every day?

The Echo

"Do to others whatever you would like them to do to you." Matthew 7:12

Tommy and his family are visiting his uncle on his farm for the holidays. Tommy is very excited. On the farm he can get up early, have lots of space to run and play games, and go for walks in nature.

One morning he went for a walk to the edge of a deep ravine. He shouted loudly: "Here I am! Hooray!"

To his surprise a boy who sounded just like him answered: "Here I am! Hooray!"

Tommy was annoyed. He thought there was a boy hiding in the valley mocking him.

So he shouted, "Stop it!"

And can you believe it, the boy shouted back, "Stop it!"

Now Tommy was angry.

He kept on shouting at the boy, but each time the voice shouted the same thing back.

Tommy went home and told the grownups about the rude little boy hiding in the ravine. Then his dad told him that the voice was his own – his echo.

That night as he lay in his bed he thought that he should've shouted, "I like you!" and then hear the voice shouting, "I like you!"

When we want someone to be friendly to us, we must be friendly and kind to them first.

Lord Jesus, thank You for teaching me to treat others well. Help me to do this. Amen.

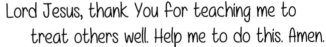

This week, make sure that you say only good and encouraging things to others.

Brothers and Sisters

How wonderful and pleasant it is when
brothers live together in harmony! Psalm 133:1

Brothers and sisters often fight with each other. Because they live in the same house and see each other all the time, some of the things that a sibling does can irritate the others. If your younger brother sings along with the radio, you feel like hitting him on the head. However, if he sits quietly in a corner, you wonder what's wrong.

Maybe you fight with your sister because you think your mom favors her more. It's unlikely that this is the case. Your mom loves all her children in her own special way. Your sister might do well in her subjects at school and your mom praises her for it. You're good at sports, which also makes your mom proud.

Each person has something special that they are good at. Don't try to be someone else. Be yourself. Praise others when they do well; admire their new outfit instead of being jealous.

Love can fix many things. Don't wait for your brother or sister to be nice and kind to you first. Be the first to say and do nice things for them. Keep doing this, even if you don't see results immediately.

Your home is the place where you practice how to treat others. When love lives in your home, it will also walk with you out the door!

Dear Jesus, give me patience and love to
treat my brothers and sisters well. Amen.

The Race of Life

Let us run with endurance the race God has set before us. We do this by keeping our eyes on Jesus, the champion who initiates and perfects our faith. Hebrews 12:1-2

A group of elementary school boys took part in a bicycle race. They had to cycle four times around the athletics field. The spectators were standing around the field cheering them on. David was in front. Everybody shouted and clapped. David's dad felt very proud.

However, David thought he only had to cycle around the field twice. After the second round he threw up his hands in the air like he had seen successful cyclists do when they won a race. He got off his bike and started to take off his shoes. By the time he realized that he had stopped halfway through, it was too late.

That day David learned an important lesson: You're finished when you complete the whole race.

The Bible also tells us about a race – the race of life. And, just like David's bicycle race, we must endure until the very end. At the finishing line Jesus is waiting for us. He doesn't mind who comes first. He just wants us to complete the race.

Dear Jesus, thank You for encouraging me
all the time in the race of life. Help me to never
give up, but to endure until the very end. Amen.

When you ride on your bike,
remind yourself that your
life is a race for God.

God Walks before Us

Our adventure with God is special. He promises to protect us from all sides.

God the Father is our rock and safe hiding place. He is like a good father. You can sit on His lap and hide when you're scared.

Jesus Christ is our Light. He shows us the way. Through His death on the cross He brought light to a dark world. Now we can see which way to go.

Until Jesus returns one day, **the Holy Spirit is with us. He is our Friend and Comforter.**

> O LORD, You have examined my heart and know everything about me. You know when I sit down or stand up. You know my thoughts even when I'm far away. You see me when I travel and when I rest at home. You know everything I do. You know what I am going to say even before I say it, LORD. You go before me and follow me. You place Your hand of blessing on my head.
>
> **Psalm 139:1-5**

The Battleship

I obey Your word instead of following a way that leads to trouble. Psalm 119:101 CEV

The *USS Montana* is a big American battleship that was built in 1905. On one occasion it had to sail along the Irish coast. Suddenly the crew saw the light of another ship right in front of them. They sent an urgent call to the ship to move to the left. The message came back: "We can't go off course. We request you to adapt your course to the right."

The captain was furious. "This is the captain of the biggest battleship in the United States of America. I instruct you to immediately move out of the way!"

The reply came back: "This is the lighthouse. We can't move."

The captain was silent. He commanded his crew to steer the ship away from the rocks where the lighthouse stood.

We do the same with God, don't we? We think that we are in charge of our own lives. Then we tell Him what to do so that we don't get into trouble. We talk with Him as if we are God and He must jump at our commands!

God is always present: steadfast and strong like a lighthouse. He shows us where the danger areas are so that we can steer clear in time.

Dear Father, thank You for being a lighthouse for me.
Thank You for protecting me from trouble and danger. Amen.

The Name of the Lord

"Our Father in heaven, may Your name be kept holy." Matthew 6:9

In movies nowadays one often hears the Lord's name being used in vain. The actors don't even think about Him when they blaspheme using His name.

When you use God's name in vain, then you are actually saying, "Oh well! I don't think much of You. You mean nothing to me." You are being disrespectful and don't acknowledge Him as King of creation.

The first of the Ten Commandments that God gave to Moses on Mount Sinai was this: "I am the Lord your God, who rescued you from the land of Egypt, the place of your slavery." (Exod. 20:2).

A bit further on it says: "You must not misuse the name of the Lord your God. The Lord will not let you go unpunished if you misuse His name" (Exod. 20:7).

These are not the words of people. No, they are God's direct commands. He wants us to understand how omnipotent and holy He is.

He wants us to respect and honor His name and worship Him. He is Almighty God and He wants us to understand this.

That's why He commands us: "You must not misuse the name of the Lord."

In biblical times the Israelites were not even allowed to say God's name out loud.

God is holy. We may never think God is our buddy or talk about Him in a disrespectful manner. God is God.

Lord God, You are all-powerful and great.
Your name is holy. Amen.

Find God's names in
Matthew 6:5-15 and
highlight or underline it.

Praise Him Every Day

Come, let us sing to the LORD! Let us shout joyfully to the Rock of our salvation. Let us come to Him with thanksgiving. Let us sing psalms of praise to Him. For the LORD is a great God, a great King above all gods. Psalm 95:1-3

Have you seen how kittens lick their front paws in order to clean themselves? Or how baby birds open their mouths wide when the mother bird returns to the nest with food? How about when your little sister or brother starts crawling on their own?

Our heavenly Father who made us is the One who enables everything to happen. We should never say: *I'm so clever, or fast or strong or pretty.* Everything we have comes from God. Therefore, we must use our talents in such a way that we bring glory to God's name.

When you achieve a good mark in an exam, first thank Jesus for giving you a sound mind. When you sing or perform well, it gladdens God's heart when you genuinely thank Him for the gifts and talents He has given you.

In Psalm 8 we read about children and babies praising the Lord. What a wonderful Father we have! We should praise Him every day for His goodness. Everything we have comes from Him!

Lord, You are the Creator of every living thing.
Thank You for blessing me with gifts. Teach me to
do everything to glorify Your name. Help me never to think
that I'm entitled to anything or that I deserve anything. Amen.

The Silversmith

He will sit as a refiner and purifier of silver; He will purify the Levites and refine them like gold and silver. Malachi 3:3 NIV

A silversmith is someone who makes jewelry and other silverware. Before he can make something out of a piece of silver, he must put it over an open flame to melt. Today silversmiths use a blowtorch to melt the silver. The flame then burns away all the impurities and only the silver remains.

The silversmith must sit there the whole time, with his eyes fixed on the piece of silver in front of him. If he looks away even for a moment, the silver can overheat and be destroyed.

A silversmith knows when the silver is purified: It's when he can see his own face in it.

God is the Silversmith of our lives. He wants to purify us from our sins that make us dull and meaningless. Therefore He holds us over a flame like precious silver. It's not always a nice feeling when the flame burns away all the impurities, but God does this because He loves us. He doesn't look away for one second. He sits there like the silversmith, until He can see His own reflection in the silver. Then He takes us out of the fire.

We often wonder why we suffer or why things go wrong, but we don't have to guess any more. It's the Lord who is busy purifying His silver so that we can be clean and reflect Him to others.

Thank You, Lord Jesus, that You want to purify me from my sins so that I can be a precious and shiny piece of silver. Amen.

A Safe Shelter

I run to You, Lord, for protection. Don't disappoint me. Psalm 71:1 CEV

One winter holiday, a bunch of cousins went to visit their grandfather on his farm. They decided to build a house from grass, in which they could play. For two days they cut long pieces of grass and put it on a pile. The bigger boys cut straight branches for the frame of the house. Then they fastened the grass with thin wire to the frame. They were very proud of their handiwork. Inside it was nice and cozy.

The children used wooden stumps as chairs. They also made a table with planks so they could eat lunch in their grass house. They were busy making plans the whole time to make their house better. That night they all went to bed with happy hearts. Life was good.

The next morning they set out excitedly for their grass shelter. From far off they saw a herd of cows grazing quietly on their grass house! There was a big hole in the roof and walls. Their cozy grass house was ruined. Their safe shelter was gone.

When the Lord tells us in the Bible that He is our safe hiding place, He really means it. When we are sad or scared or lonely, we can hide with Him. Nothing will ever destroy that shelter.

Dear Jesus, thank You that I can hide with You.
I know I'm safe there, no matter what happens. Amen.

The Tale of Mother Cat

"You did not choose Me, but I chose you and appointed you." John 15:16

A while ago I read the following story in a newspaper:

On a farm there was a cat whose kittens were due to be born any day. Just before they were born, two goose eggs hatched in the barn among the straw. The cat immediately adopted the goslings as her own. She picked them up with her mouth and carried them to safety. They crawled in under her to get warm, just like they would do with a goose.

When the kittens were born, the goslings and the kittens slept together. The goslings even tried to drink milk from the cat like the kittens did, even though geese are not mammals.

Everywhere that Mother Cat went, the goslings and kittens followed. Later the goslings grew bigger than the cat, but they still followed her around.

Just like the cat that chose the goslings, looked after them and protected them, in the same way God first chose us to be His children. He walks before us. He doesn't care who we are or where we come from or what others say about us. His love is unconditional. This means that we don't have to do anything to deserve His love. We must just follow Him.

Dear heavenly Father, thank You that I can
be Your child. Thank You for loving me first. Help
me to follow You every day of my life. Amen.

"I'm with You"

"Don't be afraid! I am with you." Isaiah 43:5 CEV

Do you get scared sometimes? Of the dark? Or that you will forget everything you've learned in the middle of an exam? Maybe you're scared that something bad will happen to your parents. Or perhaps you're afraid that your divorced parents won't love you anymore.

There are many things to be scared of. The list can be long. We hear about car accidents, children who become sick, airplanes that crash, earthquakes and floods that cause immense damage.

It's enough to scare any child. In Psalm 23, David wrote: "Even when I walk through the darkest valley, I will not be afraid, for You are close beside me."

Jesus doesn't say that there will never be tough times. What He does promise is that He will be with you. In good times and in bad times, He will take care of you.

Underline Isaiah 41:10 in your Bible. Say it out loud when you feel scared: "Don't be afraid, for I am with you. Don't be discouraged, for I am your God. I will strengthen you and help you. I will hold you up with My victorious right hand."

Dear Lord, thank You for always being with me, even when I'm sad or afraid. You promise to never leave me. That's why I can wake up every morning and not be afraid. Amen.

Learn Isaiah 41:10 off by heart.

Doubly Mine!

"All that I have is Yours, and all that You have is Mine, and they will bring glory to Me." John 17:10 CEV

Darryl lives in a town close to a river. In summertime the boys often play in the water. They swing with ropes over the river or row in canoes to the island in the middle. The smaller boys play with leaves or pieces of wood in the water to see how far they can float.

Darryl decided to make a boat that could float to a bridge in the distance. He carved a sailboat from wood and painted it white and blue. It even had a sail. His own boat!

Darryl's friends watched as he put his boat in the water. The boat slowly set sail, then went faster and faster. Everybody clapped. Then suddenly the boat slipped underneath the bridge. It was gone! Darryl was sad. His beautiful boat was lost.

Two weeks later he walked passed a secondhand shop. There in the shop window he saw his boat. He ran home and took all his savings to buy his boat back. "Now you're doubly mine. I made you and then I bought you!"

This is just like our relationship with God. He made us; then He bought us back through His Son, Jesus Christ, who died on the cross for our sins.

Thank You, Lord, that I belong to You twice.
I'm so glad that I can be Your child. Amen.

What can you do to show others how glad you are that you're a child of God?

The Lifeguard

He has made all of this plain to us by the
appearing of Christ Jesus, our Savior. 2 Timothy 1:10

When you catch the right wave and surf all the way to the beach, it makes you very excited. Later your teeth are chattering from the cold, but you don't want to stop. You tell yourself, *Just one more wave*. When you come crushing down on the sand you think, *Just one more* ... And another and another.

John and Abe played the whole morning in the water. Later they were so tired that they lay down on the surfboards. They rowed out deep where the water was quiet and floated gently along.

They enjoyed floating back and forth so much that they didn't notice the tide was pulling them towards the rocks. Only when Abe saw someone on the beach waving their hands, did he realize they were in trouble. They were too tired to swim to the beach and had to cling to their surfboards as they waited for the lifeguard.

The rocks came closer and closer. Above the noise of the water, the lifeguard said, "Hold on. Don't look down. I'm coming."

Jesus is also saying this to us today. He came to save us from our sins and to give us life in abundance. Now we can live forever with Him!

Dear Lord Jesus, You protect me from
danger and save me from sin. Thank You
for being my Lifeguard. Amen.

The Owl Box

"There is more than enough room in My Father's home. If this were not so, would I have told you that I am going to prepare a place for you?" John 14:2

At night a big owl sits in the tree in our yard. When it gets dark, he calls his mate with a deep, slow "hoo-hoo." After a while another owl answers.

Because of this, we decided to build an owl box. The beautiful box stands on a pole in our yard, hidden between the branches of a tree.

Every day we check to see if there was any movement in the box. But, no, the owls won't nest there.

It was winter and it was cold. Sometimes it rained for days on end, but the owl box stayed empty. One day, while I was listening to the owls' calls, I thought: *Owls are just like people!*

God promises us the very best. He assures us of His protection and love. However, we often think we know better, and want to do things our way. We forget the wonderful things the Lord has already done for us: His Son died for us on the cross. Our sins are washed clean. He promises us eternal life.

We must just come to Him. We are so silly and stubborn sometimes – just like the owls!

Lord Jesus, You invite me to come and live
with You and enjoy a life of abundance. Help me
to accept Your gift with outstretched arms. Amen.

The Silly Sailors

"Those who drink the water I give will never be thirsty again. It becomes a fresh, bubbling spring within them, giving them eternal life." John 4:14

I read about a small fishing boat that got into trouble in the deep sea. A storm blew them off course and they lost their oars. The four men were bobbing around on the ocean for days and they had no fresh water to drink.

Then a big ship appeared on the horizon. Finally the crew noticed the little boat and pulled closer. When they reached the ship, the sailors let down a rope ladder. The men, with sunburned faces and chapped lips, wanted nothing else but water.

"But don't you know that you're surrounded by fresh water?" asked the sailors.

"How is that possible? This is the open sea," the men replied.

"Yes, but we are in the part of the ocean where the mighty Amazon River joins the sea. All the water here is fresh – for hundreds of kilometers!"

The men let down a bucket into the water and tasted it. Sure enough, the water was sweet and fresh. To think that they had almost died of thirst while they were surrounded by fresh drinking water!

We often look for the Water of Life in the wrong places, while Jesus Christ wants to give it to us for free. We must just bend down and scoop it up.

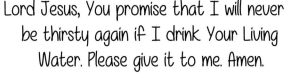

Lord Jesus, You promise that I will never be thirsty again if I drink Your Living Water. Please give it to me. Amen.

The Scared Mouse

Jesus replied, "I am the bread of life. Whoever comes to Me will never be hungry again. Whoever believes in Me will never be thirsty." John 6:35

Charles Spurgeon was a well-known British preacher and writer from the nineteenth century. He liked to tell fables. A fable is a short story, typically with animals as characters, that conveys a lesson about life. So Spurgeon told the history of Joseph in the Bible with a fable ...

Joseph was put in charge of the whole land. He commanded the Egyptians to build large barns to store grain after God revealed to him that there would be seven years of famine.

One day a small mouse appeared at Joseph's feet. Joseph looked down and asked the mouse what was wrong. The mouse nervously replied that he was worried there might not be enough grain for him.

Joseph chuckled, because the mouse would never be able to eat all the stored grain. He assured the mouse that there would be more than enough food for everyone, including the mouse and his family.

Sometimes we also get unnecessarily worried about things. We only see the hardships in our lives and forget that God cares for us.

However, He doesn't just provide us with clothes and food. He also promises that we will never be hungry or thirsty again if we believe in Him. He will feed our souls – the deepest longings of our hearts. We must just stretch out our hand and eat!

Dear Jesus, thank You for the promise that I will never be hungry or thirsty again if I come to You. Thank You for feeding me with the Bread of Life. Amen.

Next time you eat a slice of bread, think about Jesus, who is the Bread of Life.

Life Is Tweet!

Jesus Christ is the same yesterday, today, and forever. Hebrews 13:8

Children of today are smart and fast thinking. They get the hang of a new smartphone in a very short time. Sometimes your mom might ask you to fix something for her on the computer. Your fingers fly over the keyboard and before Mom can say, "Oh boy!" you've fixed the problem.

You are a child of the new era of technology and electronic marvels. If you want to find out about something, you send a text message. If you want to say something, you use Twitter.

Still, deep inside your heart you probably feel the same as children fifty years ago: shy, somewhat unsure, a little scared of grownups or older children at school. You feel bad when your friend is nasty, or if you don't get good grades. Sometimes, when you're feeling down, you just want your mom to hold you and tell you she loves you.

You can – just like those children from long ago – learn how precious it is to tell Jesus everything that goes on in your heart. His smartphone is always switched on and the battery never dies. He answers immediately when you send Him a message. Even if you don't hear His voice, He is there. He gives you the answer using the Bible, through a member of your church, or speaking to you when you pray.

Thank You, Jesus, for always
being there for me. I never have to
wonder if You've received my messages. Amen.

The Door of Your Heart

"Look! I stand at the door and knock. If you hear My voice and open the door, I will come in, and we will share a meal together as friends." Revelation 3:20

What will you do if someone knocks on your door today and it's a king in smart clothes, asking, "May I come in?"

Maybe you'll say, "Ah, no, I really don't feel like opening the door right now. Go and ask next door."

Or perhaps, "I really want you to come in but my room is very untidy. Can you come back tomorrow?"

What if the king is persistent and says, "Look, the whole street is full of trucks with beautiful furniture, jewelry and clothes. If I can come in, it's all yours"? Will you still refuse to let them in, or will your heart beat so fast with excitement that you will forget about the untidy room?

Jesus Christ is standing at the door of your life today. He asks, "Can I please come in? I want to live here. If you say 'yes,' you will inherit everything that belongs to Me."

Jesus is waiting for you to invite Him in. It's that easy. All you have to say is: "Yes, Lord, I open the door of my life to You."

Then Christ becomes part of your life. You become a child of the King of the Universe! And you inherit everything that belongs to Him, now and forever!

Dear Jesus, thank You for standing at the door of my life and knocking. Please come into my heart and live in me. Amen.

Someone to Comfort You

When the Lord saw the woman, He felt sorry
for her and said, "Don't cry!" Luke 7:13 CEV

We've all felt sad at some point. Maybe your friend doesn't want to play with you anymore. Or your teacher reprimanded you for something you didn't do. Maybe you didn't make the football or hockey team. Or you weren't chosen as a prefect. You might be feeling down and have no one to talk to about your loneliness and fears. Maybe you are mad at your parents because you feel your life is a mess, but you can't tell them. What now?

The Bible invites you to bring your sorrows to Jesus. Even if you can't see Him, you can talk to Him. Everything that bothers you, you can tell Him.

You can even write down your sadness, sorrows and unhappiness in a notebook. Tell Jesus everything that is in your heart. He will understand.

Dear Jesus, You are my Friend. You say that I can bring anything that bothers me to You. I give my sadness and sorrows to You. Help me, please. Show me what to do so that I can be better. And, if there's nothing I can do, help me to be patient and to know: You see me and You'll never forsake me. Help me through this difficult time.
Amen.

Like the Wind

"The wind blows wherever it wants. Just as you can hear the wind
but can't tell where it comes from or where it is going, so you
can't explain how people are born of the Spirit." John 3:8

A Grade 1 teacher once asked her class if they knew where wind comes from. The children's hands all went up.

"High trees swing their branches back and forth, and this is how they make wind," one boy said.

"Wind starts out at sea. Then it blows to the land," another one tried.

"I think the wind is kept in a deep cave in the mountains where no one can see it," said a dreamy eyed little girl.

Jesus tells us that we don't know where the wind begins or where it is going. It is a wonderful mystery of creation.

In the same way, we don't know how the Holy Spirit works. It's like a wind that blows through us and fills us with the Lord's love and goodness.

When we allow Christ into our lives, we open the door of our heart to the Holy Spirit, which is where He wants to be. If He dwells in our hearts He becomes our Comforter, Friend and Teacher. The Holy Spirit teaches us every day how to live. We must just allow Him to do His work.

Holy Spirit, please blow into my heart and life.
Fill me to the brim. I want to learn from You
how to live a life that honors God. Amen.

Cool Beans

"You know the Spirit, who is with you and will keep on living in you." John 14:17 CEV

There is an easy way to see how a bean sprouts. Take a saucer and a piece of cotton wool. Put three big beans on top of the cotton wool and cover it with another piece. Make the cotton wool damp and then put the saucer on the window sill in the sun. Water it every day.

Lift the top piece of cotton wool regularly to see if the beans have sprouted. Can you believe it! After a few days you can see the sprouts. Later you will even see green leaves. You can't do anything; you can just wait for the bean plants to grow.

When you look at beans in this way, you realize that it can only be God who grows the bean sprouts. Usually this happens in the ground – where no one can see it.

When you give your heart and life over to Jesus, God starts His invisible and secret work in you, like the beans quietly grow inside the cotton wool. The Holy Spirit dwells in you and even though you cannot see Him, He is always with you to comfort and teach you.

Dear Lord Jesus, I want the Holy Spirit
to be in my life. Work in my heart so
that I can be a child of Yours. Amen.

Grow some beans at home, as
described in the experiment above.

Fiery Tongues

Then they saw what looked like fiery tongues moving in all directions, and a tongue came and settled on each person there. The Holy Spirit took control of everyone. Acts 2:3-4 CEV

After Jesus ascended to heaven, the disciples were very sad. They didn't know how to carry on without their Teacher. They forgot what He said the night before His crucifixion. Jesus had encouraged them. He had told them, "I will ask the Father to send you the Holy Spirit who will help you and always be with you" (John 14:16 CEV).

The Holy Spirit comforts us. Even today He is with us, Jesus' children. He helps us to pray when we don't know how to pray. He comforts us and takes our worries away. He helps us to show God to our friends who don't know Him through the way we live.

When the Holy Spirit came down on the disciples, there were fiery tongues on their heads. Through this God wanted to show that when we allow the Holy Spirit into our life, He will strengthen us and help us shine bright in the world.

We are so privileged! We have a Father who loves each one of us. We have His Son, Jesus Christ, who died for our sins, and we have the Holy Spirit who teaches us and looks after us until Jesus returns one day.

Dear Father, Son and Holy Spirit, I'm just a child and I don't always understand everything. Thank You for making me feel safe, because I know that You will take care of me for all eternity. Amen.

God's Blessing

May the LORD bless you and protect you. May the LORD smile on you and be gracious to you. May the LORD show you His favor and give you His peace. Numbers 6:24-26

The Lord's wish for each of His children is that it will go well with them.

When you read in the Bible how Solomon blessed the Israelites after they dedicated the temple to God, you hear this same blessing. He pleads: "May the LORD our God be with us as He was with our ancestors; may He never leave us or abandon us" (1 Kings 8:57).

Every Sunday before leaving church, the pastor blesses the congregation.

The word *bless* has such a wonderful meaning. The Hebrew word for *bless* is *barag*. It means to kneel in respect before someone whom you want to bless and offer a gift to.

That's what I want to do with every word in this devotional. I want to give you a backpack full of God's words, to help you every day. I pray that He will bless you with every word.

Dear Father, I pray that every child reading this book will be blessed and protected. Keep them safe on their journey. Always be the One walking in front. Show them the dangers and help them to be obedient. May they always remember that You are with them every step of the way. Amen.

Find the treasure!

Store your treasures in heaven, where moths and rust cannot destroy, and thieves do not break in and steal. Wherever your treasure is, there the desires of your heart will also be. Matthew 6:20-21

Jesus is buried

This word puzzle is especially for youngsters. Use the words to tell them about the special tomb Jesus was buried in — the one He didn't remain in. You can read this part of the Easter story in Luke 23:50-56.

			J	E	S	U	S	
			E	N	E	B	A	
			R	O	C	Y	B	
			U	P	I	Z	B	

C	R	O	S	S	P	P	L	A	M	K	W	A
M	U	G	J	A	R	S	O	T	I	T	E	U
U	R	E	X	L	L	E	I	H	F	H	I	J
R	J	O	S	E	P	H	N	X	T	O	M	B

M	B	O	T	A
L	Q	U	M	I
I	F	I	E	G
O	R	I	N	O
A	I	R	T	B
F	D	E	R	Y
W	A	L	D	A
H	Y	D	O	B
Y	S	X	E	L

Words to find

JESUS

BODY

OINTMENT

JERUSALEM

JOSEPH

SPICES

FRIDAY

TOMB

CROSS

ARIMATHEA

SABBATH

LAW

God gives light and warmth

The LORD, my God, lights up my darkness. Psalm 18:28

Answers